Seasons to taste
Field to table, past to present

A story of food in the Peak District

Edited by
David Fine

The Farming Life Centre

Published by:
The Farming Life Centre
Blackwell Hall Farm, Blackwell, Buxton, Derbyshire SK17 9TQ
www.thefarminglifecentre.org.uk

Cover design: Matt Watson and Damian Hughes

Book design: Dick Richardson
e-mail: dickrichardson@country-books.co.uk

Picture editor: Damian Hughes
e-mail: dphughes@dphphotography.plus.com

ISBN 978 0 955994 10 4

Printed and bound by: HSW Print

Acknowledgements

This is the page which all too soon becomes a list. Before naming names, I'd like to say how much of a pleasure it has been working with everyone, and how readily and how hard they've worked. This book has been a team effort, where my role as editor has been to bring things together as a whole, so blame for any grammatical and similar textual errors is to be laid solely at my door.

First of all, I'd like to thank the interviewees or contributors who gave up their time and spent no little effort explaining their involvement with food in one way or the other. An index of their names with 'sound-bites' is at the back of the book.

Next, the volunteers who did the interviewing, and that task of Job, transcription: Dean Biddell, Jen Bower, Mary Courtis, Damian Hughes, Mary Landon, Andréa Lewis, Tana McMeechan, Lynne Mycock and Elspeth Walker, take a bow and a big round of applause. I'd also like to thank Damian who took many of the photographs and has also done a tremendous job in the role of picture editor to ensure that what you see is at least as satisfying as what you read.

Whereas I was merely tasked with putting the words into good order, Jen Bower, Julia Cook and most recently and avidly Hannah Watson were employed by the Farming Life Centre to bring together and co-ordinate all our efforts.

Also behind the scenes have been: Tony Faulkner, who supported our volunteers on behalf of Read On – Write Away!; Colin Hyde of East Midlands Oral History Archive, who trained on the best ways to interview, record, transcribe and archive oral history; Frances Ashfield and Jen Bower, who helped put together the successful application to the Heritage Lottery Fund, which paid for all this work, including the book you're now reading; Dick Richardson of Ashridge Press, for design and print of this book; the Trustees of the Farming Life Centre for having the faith to back a fairly ambitious project; and lastly Caroline Pick, of Museums, Libraries and Archives East Midlands, for the original idea.

To you all no praise is too much, and also to my family, for being so keen and understanding, especially during two illnesses that beset me between start and finish.

David Fine, July 2008

1. The Team at Blackwell Hall Farm (the Farming Life Centre), 2008
L to R: Tony Faulkner, Andréa Lewis, Tana McMeechan, Elspeth Walker,
Damian Hughes, David Fine, Julia Cook, Mary Courtis, Lynne Mycock
and Hannah Watson.
© Damian Hughes

The team at the Farming Life Centre joins in these thanks, and of course, thanks David for the skill, and enthusiasm, with which he drew out a narrative from the many and disparate interviews.

We would also like to thank a number of people who made sourcing the illustrations for this book a much easier process: Ruth Gordon at DCC Local Studies Library; Tina Ball at REAP; Tina Bowler from the Peak District Dairy Wagon; Ben from Buxton Museum and Art Gallery; Diane Naylor at the Chatsworth Estate Library; Midlands Co-operative Society; Julie Bunting of the Peak Advertiser; and the private collections of Tom Brocklehurst, Angela Taylor, the Gregory family, the Ollerenshaw family and John Furness.

Again, we would like to add our gratitude to David's for the amazing work produced by Damian Hughes. We would also like to extend our gratitude to the other photographers who kindly gave their work, free of charge: Colin Shaw, Ken Davis, Patrick Downie, Alison Furness, Tom Jolley, Sheila Hine, Lynne Mycock, Andrea Lewis, Julia Cook, Fred Watson and Peter Miles.

And to everyone who has had a part in this story of food, whether named or not, a huge thank you from me.

Hannah Watson, Peak District Food Heritage Project Manager

Contents

Illustrations

Market

Table

Introduction

At a conference nearly four years ago I met Caroline Pick of Museums, Libraries and Archives – East Midlands. Caroline had the marvellous idea of a project which captured the oral history of food in the region. 'You're a writer,' she said, 'does it interest you?'

God knows how many slices of bread, cups of tea, breakfasts, lunches, dinners and snacks in between have passed all our lips since then – it's two-way traffic, food in and words out – but when you pause to think about things we take for granted, you appreciate how vital food and language are to how we live.

Both are apparently simple yet very complex the more you delve... I could bore you with chapter and verse about how the Romans brought chickens together with Latin to these shores, shortly after the birth of Christ, right up to the Treaty of Rome, which left us out of the Common Market fifty years ago. Oral history gives immediacy, a feel for time and place, which documents tend to push away. EU legislation is pretty dry stuff, but read Richard Gill (page 26) or Ian Lawton (page 28) on milk quotas and subsidies, and you soon appreciate the dairy farmer's struggle to turn a squirt from an udder into a healthy bank-balance, just so we can have milk, cheese, cream, yoghurt ... when we like.

'I'm sick of farmers bellyaching,' said a caller on a *Radio 5 Live* phone-in towards the end of the 2001 Foot and Mouth epidemic. 'All they have to do is put food on our table.' Excuse me. What about all the butchers, bakers, greengrocers, dairies, wholesalers, retailers, delivery drivers, shelf-stackers, check-out operators and shop assistants? And that's before anything's cooked. The sad thing about the phone-in was that no-one, not the presenter, not the minister nor the NFU rep, sought to inform the caller. That's how dislocated, broken our view of food is today.

This dislocation was something we aimed to address, if not put right. Although a history, *Seasons to Taste* isn't a sepia-tinted exercise in biscuit-tin nostalgia; if it looks backwards it is to see ahead in a world where today we throw away around a quarter of the food we put in our shopping baskets, if not on our tables. Early on in the planning we decided to scout for interviews which covered the food industry from plough to microwave in the Peak District. I think we've achieved this. In order to make a sensible story from hundreds of thousands of recorded words, we split things into three – Field, Market and Table – since these seemed to sum up the sequence from farming to eating. Or in master butcher Mick Shirt's words, "from gate to plate." You'll find each of these sections tells their story, in rough chronological order, reaching back to just after the First World War. Taken together you'll appreciate the stretch of the title, *Seasons to Taste*.

Although *Seasons to Taste* draws exclusively from the Peak District, and has a Peak District feel, I'm sure its accounts will ring bells for anyone with just a nodding acquaintance of rural and market town life – we all need to eat, and nearly all of us need to buy most of our food. For those who rarely go beyond on-line or supermarket shopping, it's a good and welcoming guide into a rich world that parallels the check-out.

When we started interviewing, the fear was we wouldn't have enough; it transpired we collected five to ten times more than could be included in a book. Editing was a ruthless procedure. It hurts to limit accounts of value and interest, a hurt only partially assuaged by the potential for including excluded material, together with recipes and remedies, on a website *www.thefarminglifecentre. org.uk/seasons_to_taste.* A further project aim is to create listening posts so you can hear excerpts of the interviews. Within the grammar of print, I've tried to retain individual voices, so you can hear them as you read, make them live.

In cutting I've tried to leave the essence of what people have said. In assembly I've tried to find a narrative. You can choose to pick-and-dip or read cover-to-cover: I imagine you'll do a bit of both. To help you along, each of the three sections has its introduction which highlights themes, just as the photo-graphs illustrate individual subjects. There's no strong editorial line, I've left that for you to determine. It's very much a history of food over the last hundred years, in the participants' own words.

A listening post, a bill of fare into the past — and future.

Field

How many of us, even if we live in the countryside, know a farmer? Statistically they've almost become an endangered species yet farmers, above all else, make the countryside itself. Field is an opportunity for you to eaves-drop on farmers, a rare privilege.

Alongside farmers, we hear from the trades which use their produce, such as Alan Salt's account of Hartington Stilton, made at the oldest cheese factory still running (page 31). A theme which runs through these accounts, as evidently as a vein in stilton, is the expertise required to make a success of things. Skills and judgements which cannot entirely be learnt from a book but only through years of experience – read Geoffrey Townsend's shepherd's year (page 38).

Perhaps not surprisingly farming skills and expertise pass from generation to generation, as the first three pieces demonstrate: Bill Chadwick's account of making a hay-rick (page 45); Mick Shirt's of the slaughter-man's art (page 53); Margaret Oven's of puncturing the stomachs of blown sheep, which could be Gabriel Oak in Hardy's Far From The Madding Crowd. With the decline of mining and heavy industries, only farming and sea-fishing, (never common in the Peak District) are passed on this way. It's not unquestioning, as Richard Gill's surprise demonstrates, when his son suggests going from dairy to water buffalo (page 25), but it's easy to see how communities build up and maintain themselves – Bill Chadwick's account of Hiring Fayres before World War II makes this clear (page 51).

Since then, the external demand to increase productivity has tested the resilience of farmers to the utmost. With fewer working on the land, loneliness at the work-place becomes more of a problem: there are fewer of them meeting less often. 'Managing risk is something that farmers have always had to cope with,' says Tony Kemish, in order to lessen the risk of supply for consumers. Today they also have to deal with the risks of the market itself where, arguably, they have less control or understanding than of natural risks. Not even governments or stock markets can do much about a credit crunch or the food shortages they create, why expect farmers to do more – especially in a business where it takes years to realise a profit. It's a world apart from being out in the field, where the time saved by mechanisation appears to have been taken up with filling in forms. As Mark Dennison says of bee-keeping. 'It's a funny sort of farming, we're not bogged down by paperwork.'

Some farmers adapt more readily than others. Small self-help groups such as the Cow Club (page 52), High Peak Livestock Society (page 53), and local initiatives like the Peak District Dairy Wagon (page 32) and the Farming Life Centre itself, enable all to get together and learn from one another in an organic network of *local communal groups. It is a very different world from how DEFRA and the EU operate. Curiously today, just at the onset of a global food shortage and not helped by the growth of bio-fuels, the powers-that-be are implementing a regime based more on quality – of the food and the environment – than productivity. As Richard Gill puts it "It's amazing how it's come round, isn't it? That we were farming organically, but didn't know it, and now we're farming organically again."*

Perhaps it's a change back for the better, a better paced way of living. As we become more environmentally aware, we will better appreciate the subtle nature of wresting food from the earth, either through plants or animals. It may have something to do with what we do to ourselves as well as the countryside. Let the sting in the tail lie with Mark Dennison's bees:-

"It's a very timeless sort of job. That's what I enjoy most. We don't use much in the way of mechanization; it's a traditional way of working and quite peaceful when you're out there with the bees working away. You have to be calm. In fact the times I get stung most is when I'm out stressed and rushing, because they feel it." (page 34)

Five Generations

I was born here. The farm house is large, seven bedrooms to it, no heating at all until father got up in the morning and lit the fire and of course it warmed the rooms. We did put in an Aga in 1949 and that transformed the kitchen. Every room had an old coal fire grate in it, even the upstairs bedrooms.

The house was built about 1870. Mr Hattersley was the tenant in those days and when he died my great-grandfather, Samuel, came down from Stoney Middleton and took over the tenancy in 1895. He died in 1908 and my great uncle Gladstone took over, then my father took over in 1928. I took over in 1960 and my son Jimmy took over about ten years ago, so we've had five generations of Furness' on the farm.

James Furness, farmer

2 'From Father to Son'. Jim and James Furness outside the farmhouse, 2008 © Colin Shaw

From Father to Son

My father used to say "Here you are, you go and do that, make your mistakes while I can afford to pay for them," and I'm afraid I took that attitude. George was buying and selling when he was fifteen. If you don't give them responsibility they don't accept it, it's as simple as that. People used to say "Don't you ring up and see how they're going on?" and I said I didn't. "If they make a mistake, they can put it right before I get back."

The boys never wanted to do anything else. One's married with three children, and the other isn't married; the one you've just seen, I can't get rid of him... My wife was a farmer's daughter. Although she worked in a bank, she never wanted to do anything else but farm, it was in her genes as you might say. She was in the land army and we were married in forty-five and she helped me. She could do anything outside as well as in. The boys never wanted to do anything else and my daughter, she got to be the manager of a bank. We always said all she did that for was to find a wealthy farmer to marry. Well, she married a farmer, she's done all right, she's quite happy.

Ray Platts, farmer

Mother and Daughter

3 Mother and Daughter. Sue and Erica Jackson, on the farm, 2008 © Damian Hughes

My parents had the chance of buying this farm in the early 1970s at a low price and at the time, like a lot of rural children, I was interested in horses, and while I was working in one of the places with horses they asked me whether I could drive a tractor, and I couldn't. But I was interested so they taught me to drive a tractor and I thought "this is better than horses because you don't fall off! And I went to agricultural college and that's how the farming started. It's always been livestock. It's an upland farm, and it's relatively small acreage, seventy-two acres. So always been livestock. I started with cattle and introduced sheep, and I've now cattle, sheep, pigs and poultry. I've changed from hay-making to haylage so it's not quite so dependent on the weather. It's all grass; we can't grow crops. The biggest implication of that has been the increase in the price of animal feed that we have to buy in. Now I own the farm."

Sue Jackson, farmer

I've got my own flock of hens, which I look after. Whenever mum needs help with the sheep work, I do that. And I just generally do jobs that one person can't do.

Erica Jackson, Sue's daughter

How farms have changed

Things are totally different now. There was no building erected here from 1863 till 1968. There was obviously not enough money to put up new buildings and then in the sixties and seventies there was plenty of money available – grants for putting up new buildings – and most farmers availed themselves of it as we did, we put a new cow shed up and put roads around the farm.

4 Meadow flowers, 2008 © Fred Watson

5 Blackwell Hall Farm in the 1930s © Courtesy of Angela Taylor from the Gregory Collection

5 Blackwell Hall Farm today, 2008 © Damian Hughes

And you had a grant for ploughing up old pasture and things like that - I'm not so sure that it was a good idea really. There was a lot of good old pasture destroyed.

We've just one, one very ancient hay meadow, full of herbs and flowers and things, but really they creep back if you don't plough them again and even if you do, it wouldn't take much encouragement to get it back. Round the walls where it's not ploughed there's a reservoir of stuff. Wild vetch and things like that. Lady's Bedstraw and Cowslips and Bladder Campion and Orchids.

Bill Gregory, farmer

Farming Today

Now the living's nothing whatsoever to do with the livestock. You couldn't live solely as a live-stocker; it's got to be out of grants, conservation grants for looking after the countryside. And that's the big change from looking after stock. A lot of these farms on the hills now are having to turn to looking after the countryside and that's pretty well the income from it.

John Eardley, farmer

Risk

Managing risk is something that farmers have always had to cope with. The Peak District might be a bit worse than others because extremes of weather can be quite different from the top end of the Peak District down to the southern end. I can certainly remember in the seventies when we had sheep on keep. In other words sheep were brought down from Wildboarclough to be grazed on the home farm and went back in good shape at the beginning of April. I think it would be about that time, about a week or two after they went back, that out of the hundred, probably fifteen of those or so got buried [in snow]. So we do have great extremes in a very short distance.

Tony Kemish, farmer

Farms: Tenanted and In-hand

- a view from the late eighties

The landlord and tenant system of land tenure is the age-old way for a man to be able to farm without having a large capital sum to invest in land and buildings as well as stock. It has stood the test of time..... A consolidating act was required and the Agricultural Holdings Act 1986 embodied all previous legislation, and is the basis on which agricultural tenancies are now administered. When agriculture prospered and the cost of new buildings and repairs were rising at the same time, the rents were reviewed every three years. Roger Wardle visited one third of the farms annually and agreed an increase in rent with the tenant. He walked the fields and surveyed the buildings with the farmer, who could rid himself of his complaints against the Wicked Landlord while at the same time Roger could see how the land was being farmed and whether the tenant was keeping up his repairing liabilities. The ritual dance which was performed each time took several hours, with bargaining and counter-bargaining over cups of tea or more – and the valuable contract between landlord and tenant was thus kept up.

The Duchess of Devonshire *The Estate: A view from Chatsworth*, Macmillan 1990 p20-21

Growing Up On A Farm

As a child through the sixties we lived on a farm at Hassop, near Bakewell, where my dad was the dairyman who worked for Sir Francis and Lady Stevenson, who owned most of the village and pretty well all you could see as far as Chatsworth. It was a good sort of life because it was as if it was you who had an estate there, and the farm was a playground, a massive playground for kids basically, so you were never short of something to do.

There were a lot of foxes around – they used to get the lambs and the sheep. I mean, I remember going down the fields and coming across sheep and lambs that were in a really dreadful mess, been torn to pieces. I remember that quite distinctly; not very nice for young kids and you'd come across it quite suddenly. There was a gamekeeper, a very good one I seem to remember but he did upset us on one occasion because we had ended up with a pigeon. We were looking after and feeding it and it stopped with us very locally around the house,

6 The farm was a playground, 2008 © Damian Hughes

flying around for weeks on end and we were certain that when it disappeared, the gamekeeper had shot it and it had a name, the pigeon, which I don't recall now but I remember we were certain he'd shot it. The gamekeeper had had his eye on it for weeks, and he shot the poor old pigeon eventually. We were certain of that - which was a bit upsetting for kids. Later on I used to be - well, attempt to be - the vermin extinguisher in terms of shooting rats. My claim to fame is I once shot fifty-odd rats in a weekend which I thought was quite an achievement at the time. It was some going when there was a particular vermin problem. I didn't need asking to do the job, oh no, I was out of control - like we just went off shooting.

But there wasn't a lot of slaughtering of animals actually on the farm. They used to go to market, though I do remember my mum asking Uncle Bill, who ran the farm, for a chicken. I don't know what it was for, Christmas or whatever but she wanted a big chicken and he said he'd get her one cause there were lots of quite big chickens on the farm. He turned up at the kitchen door with a big live hen under his arm and proceeded to wring its neck in front of my mother amidst a cloud of feathers going all round the kitchen and my mother went absolutely berserk. She thought she was going to get a plucked chicken and she actually got the live version which had its neck pulled right in front of her in the middle of the kitchen. Bill was a character and he did it to basically annoy mum as some sort of joke but she didn't find it at all amusing.

Michael Pearson, farmer's son

Three Cottages

I was born in Tideswell in 1943. I was always interested in the farm and outdoor life and started helping my dad milking when I was about ten. He taught me a lot of what I know, building walls up and things like that.

The job's worsening - it's no way to make a living unless you have a big acreage. It's just, unless you like it, it's slavery. So I didn't really encourage my own children to do a lot on the farm. They do school teaching jobs, things like that and social work. I'm sad: I have two grandsons and they both like coming round the farm with me, but they'll never be able to take it over. Because there wouldn't be enough land. You need two to three hundred acres now to make any sort of a living, with a hundred cows - the Friesen Holstein now. I've sold the cows about six years ago. Well, we'd only a small milk quota, you need a big one to carry on. I was getting older so I decided the best thing to do was get out of the cows and just keep more sheep. I've only sheep on now. They're cross-breds, Texel crosses mainly.

My great grandfather had these three houses built, you see, and my grand-father lived in one, his sister had the second one next door, although she didn't live in it, and this one was let out. My mother was born in the first cottage and then they moved to the second cottage when they were married and now we are sitting in the third cottage. Although I was born in the first house it was only because my dad was away during the war you see. My sister still lives in the first one, where I was born. I don't think people stay in the same area now, do they?

Harold Oven, farmer

7 Three Cottages - Harold and Wilf Oven (with Freda in the background), 2008 © Peter Miles

From Grazing To Table

The Peak District is more a livestock production rather than a finishing area.

Finishing means the second stage in the animal's life whereby it's not on the same farm that it started. Finishing is fattening and the fat sheep or the fat bullock goes to the market to the butcher for meat which is your food.

Sheep are sold off the grass and when the grass runs out you've got to feed them something else which we don't grow in the Peak District. That's the basis of what it's about. Lambs will be born later in the Peak District and there will be some sold as milk lambs. That's a lamb that's basically got fat off its mother's milk. The earliest Spring lambs will only be thirteen or fourteen weeks old when they're sold; your Easter lamb and Whitsuntide lamb and all the rest of it.

One of the biggest changes in the limestone area was the bringing in of water supply, because a lot of the farms were short of water. When the natural supply dried up you couldn't graze the field anymore.

8 A natural water supply - a dewpond on the limestone upland, 2008 © Damian Hughes

Mains supply mainly came after the Second World War, fifties into the sixties and made the farms up here worth a lot more, because you could graze for longer and increase yields. That was a big factor.

Ian Lawton, livestock auctioneer

Milk Marketing Board

When we had The Milk Marketing Board, you see, the government governed how much the milk would be on the doorstep or in the shops. Then the Milk Marketing Board ceased and it had the adverse effect of actually pushing the price of milk down because supermarkets could then dictate to the farmer how much they had to pay for the milk and how much they were going to pay. The price of milk went down to the farmer but it went up to the consumer, so the supermarkets were making a lot of money at the farmer's expense on that score. I actually pay direct to the farm so I pay them the price they should be getting and they're quite happy with that so anybody who buys milk off me is actually helping the farmer as well. If you buy off a supermarket, you're only helping the supermarket not the farm. So it is politically wrong, there's no doubt about it.

Pauline Jackson, milk lady

When The Milk Marketing Board was formed in the thirties it gave security. There were a lot of small dairy farms in the area, which, as everybody knows now, are

9 The milk wagon in the 1930s – security of supply under the Milk Marketing Board
© Courtesy of Angela Taylor from the Gregory Collection

shrinking. The numbers of dairy producers are shrinking by the day, and the biggest nail in the coffin for the dairy farmer was de-regulation where they took away the Milk Marketing Board, which negotiated a price with the dairies and it gave them power. I don't like the use of the word power but it gave them enough negotiating power with the people to whom they were selling milk. The free market now works because the government felt it should. It's politics and there's too much politics in food. Milk production is a huge pyramid. You've got Tesco and ASDA[1] and these people at the top and then you've got thirty odd thousand milk producers, so it's a pyramid. And the one on top of the pyramid's the most powerful, aren't they?

Farmers also get less today because about forty odd percent is now liquid consumption. The rest of it goes into butter and cheese and the price for butter and cheese milk is much less than the liquid price. Also, the weight of export milk imported into the country because we are the sort of dustbin of the world for everybody.

Ian Lawton, livestock auctioneer

————

1. ASDA stands for Associated Dairies and Farm Stores Limited, formed in 1949 from a dairy farmers-led partnership after WWI to help secure good price for their produce. How the wheel turns.

From Organic To Organic

I am a stockman. You know on my gravestone I hope it will say "stockman." And to this day, you see, it breaks my heart when I've had to sell the cows. But we'll get to that in a while.

I can remember when I was ten being in this farm kitchen with no electricity, no water, no telephone and it was really like going back a hundred years. All we had was Tilley lamps. You'd pump them up and you'd have these mantles to light, which was one of my jobs when I got home from school. Used to hate it on a cold October, November evening, father and mum out working on the farm and there was always a note to say it was my job to light the Tilley lamps. I used to go down to my friends in Chesterfield and watch the TV and be fascinated by electricity where you'd press a button and the light would come on. Then all at once within ten years we were sat in our sitting rooms watching a TV and a man walking on the moon. Incredible.

At school I was very interested in farming and business. I stress the business side of farming because the two don't necessarily go together. Farmers can be very good farmers but not particularly good businessmen – so when I left school I realised that I had to further my education and maybe streamline it towards agriculture because agriculture was just starting to blossom. I'm talking now about the mid-sixties. By 1968 I left Broomfield Agricultural College very young and enthusiastic and realised that we'd got to make a lot of milk. At that particular time I was very lucky because the government was doing some grant schemes. It enabled us to transform our way of farming which was still like it was maybe a hundred years ago. We'd only 140 acres and bearing in mind that we were farming one of the highest farms in the Peak District, eleven hundred feet above sea level. So that limited what I could do, what I could grow. We were growing a few potatoes. Kept about ten pigs and twenty cows and some hens which were my mum's money, turkeys for Christmas, a few geese and it all went to make a balanced farm. The

10 The Tilley Lamp, 2008
© Hannah Watson

ironic thing is that we were farming organically but we didn't know it.

Of course, I mean, I realised that we had to change, we had to get more, dare I say it, factory farming – I'd spent time at college and learned how to use fertilisers to grow grass and grass varieties and all at once we were using artificial insemination and were doubling the amount of milk yield per cow. It was exciting, really exciting for me. I was proud of what we were doing. We were feeding people and we put in these milking parlours and started to breed Holsteins, put in some buildings, acquired more land. For the first time ever we went into an overdraft situation which my father, never had any money, but he'd die if he thought that he owed anybody any money. He would live within his means. It was very difficult for me to actually change his views.

We got rid of the sheep, what few sheep we had. All the hens had gone. We had high rainfall which led to grass production and I've always prided myself on growing good crops of grass and even at eleven hundred feet we were growing two or three a year, which didn't help the wildlife I may add, especially with the ground nesting birds, which we were rapidly destroying because it never gave them chance to nest. We were taking a cut of silage in the last week in May when the birds had just got some young ones and then you'd put a mower straight through the field and you'd chop up everything. They'd just build again and have a new nest and that was just in time for the second cut. So we were rapidly destroying the wildlife. But we kept going and then disaster struck in 1983.

11 Spring cut for silage, 2008 © Damian Hughes

Milk Quotas

The EU brought in milk quotas, which was one of the most ridiculous and unfair ways of doing this because people like myself had spent a massive amount of money into all these buildings to make milk and were totally grass orientated, all at once we were caught in this trap and I think my milk quota was 420,000 litres! It was absolutely ridiculous! We couldn't make a living on that. I'd put everything in to do at least double that and my hands were tied. A lot of cows had to be slaughtered; we couldn't employ anyone. We struggled on for a few years until they made milk quota transferable so we started to buy milk quota, which enabled us to get back to where we were. To be honest, with hindsight, you could make more money leasing and buying and selling quota than what you could actually doing an honest day's work and producing the milk. It's another of those ridiculous situations. We muddled on and slowly built a reasonable quota until the mid-nineties. After the next crisis, the 2001 foot and mouth, like the BSE, stock went very scarce and it enabled me to sell at an inflated price. It enabled me to build up enough funds to go out and say, well we need to do something else. Richard was still at university, and I left him here with the herdsman and about a hundred cows while Jennifer, my wife, and I bought The Nag's Head in Castleton.

Water Buffalo

We were still farming here, but of course all the time inflation's going up and the price of milk stagnated, it's held at about 18p, 17p and we were starting to really struggle. We were employing a herdsman for thirty years and to pay his wages and to pay everything else and I'm thinking "This doesn't make a lot of sense." Richard of course, he came, and again sometimes you bring your kids up and you teach them to be businessmen but sometimes you don't like the information that you're going to get. For years we'd developed a lovely herd of cows because every time we had a herd sale we'd keep the cream so you were actually improving the quality of the herd all the time. He said "Well this doesn't make a lot of sense. I'm not interested in milking cows. I can't see things dramatically changing." We had to start looking for other things.

"Water Buffalo," he suggested.

"A what?!"

"A Water Buffalo. I'm going to go to a farmers' market."

Up until then farmers' market had always been – I thought – you know, amateurs-ville. But he arranged for this water buffalo to come onto the farm and to take it to one of the local farmers' markets. The thing was to get into a niche market that no one else was in. Richard sent me out; I did nothing for about nine months but run round the country buying buffalo. We started with six and now, to cut a long story short, we run about three-seventy head of buffalo. Three and a half

12 Water buffalo in a Peak District meadow, 2008 © Damian Hughes

years ago in the first six months we did about 12,000 burgers, which I thought was quite reasonable. Last year we did 68,000. To date this year we've done just over a 100,000 so we're hoping to finish at around 125,000. I use the burger loosely because that's just a rule of thumb as to how the rest is doing. We also do sausage. Incidentally our garlic and herb sausage just won the Bakewell Show.

Return To Organic

I suppose that's where really agriculture's come, in that we've had to turn into business people rather than just do a job. Those that do a job and produce a good honest living making milk and beef are really struggling. We went out of milk and sold the whole herd in 2004. We applied for Higher Level Stewardship which means we've got to farm in an environmentally sensitive way. We reckoned if we're going to take Higher Level Stewardship we may as well make the organic conversion. Now we're farming for subsidies but we're doing a good job in so much that we are actually increasing the number of lapwings and other birds and that's one of the reasons why the buffalo has had to go. They wouldn't fit alongside the Higher Level Stewardship. I'm just going to keep maybe a hundred organic Aberdeen Angus cattle, basically just to keep it tidy. And of course, Angus is superb beef, and we'll put it through our own shop. We're just bringing the whole farm down to a level that can sustain itself really, if that makes sense. We don't have to put any fertiliser or anything else on. It just keeps a hundred head of cattle.

It's amazing how it's come round isn't it? That we were farming organically, but didn't know it, and now we're farming organically again. It seems an awful long way since those very cold nights in the early sixties with no electricity or water and the Tilley Lamps to light but when I look over the last 40 years it's been a wonderful, incredible ride.

Richard Gill, farmer

Organic vs. Non-organic

Everyone sees organic and non-organic as good versus bad but there's more to it than that. It's fair to say generally with organic farming you are not going to get the yields that you'd get from a non-organic farm. The flip side is you've also not generally got the input costs of a non-organic farm where you are generally applying fertilizer, spraying off the weeds and they have a cost both in buying the bio-chemicals plus the labour and machinery. We always get asked the question "Why is organic food more expensive then?"

Generally you are not getting as much per acre as you were with a non-organic system. It's an acknowledgement that you are putting a lot of fertilizer on to make the grass grow quicker; you are cutting the silage; you are feeding corn to cattle to get them fatter quicker and that's not just a difference between organic and non-organic, it's as much the difference between intensive and extensive methods.

For National Trust tenants we would support them going organic in that we will pay for registration fees and all first year costs of registering with an organic certification body as well as giving advice, but as I've said a number of times it's more about the conservation and land management as a whole. A fair part of my role is building up a good relationship with our tenants so we do things by negotiation to improve conservation and wildlife values.

Russell Ashfield, National Trust

In The Milk Shed

I used to do all the feeding and basically we had this big barn by the side of the milk sheds and we used to mix all the feeds up. We had a great big chart on the wall and each cow would have her name and the amount of feed she was expected to have and we would mix it accordingly and I had to take responsibility from a very, very young age to do that. I often used to fall in the big tub of feed where it was all mixed and everything but, you know, it was something I enjoyed doing. We used to creep up between the cattle, nothing like there is today, you fed in a manger in front of the cattle so you had to walk behind, then between the two of them, feed them, give them a cuddle and a tickle behind their horns and things like this. I would help empty units, strain the milk into the churns and in the summer we'd have a big cooling trough where we'd put the milk in for cooling and they were collected by a lorry from the Co-op in Sheffield. He used to come every morning to collect the churns and that would be the end of the milking session in the mornings.

Jill Horton, farmer's daughter

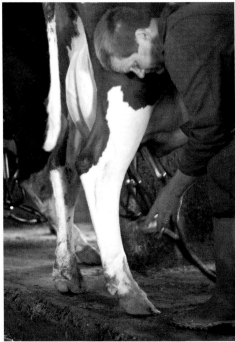

13 In the Milking Shed, Blackwell Hall Farm, 2008 © Damian Hughes

EU – before and after

After the war there was the 'forty-seven Agricultural Act. The best minister we ever had was a local, Tom Williams, born in Blackwell. I was only a child at the time. It brought protection for the tenant farmers. If his landlord didn't like him he couldn't kick him out. They had a protected tenancy provided they farmed to certain standards. They brought about the support price for most of the commodities and that produced stability in farming. I suppose the best years in farming would be the fifties and sixties. They'd be the best twenty years in the last hundred years from a point of view of stability, profit and lifestyle and all the rest of it. But it was a very efficient system before we went into the common market. They had a guaranteed price. If the guarantee price is a pound and the market price is ten shillings, the ten shillings he is paying to the producer as a tax, he's having the benefit of it because he's buying it at ten shillings a pound. It's not rocket science. It's as simple as that. And you didn't have a surplus that you had to pay to store. You had a bit of paperwork and you paid the farmer. End of story, no surpluses on to the next year.

Then we went into the common market and did it the European way. Keep the market price up and you buy it off the market. It has cost billions of pounds, euros, whatever and it doesn't achieve because you get people producing stuff like wine lakes and butter mountains and it doesn't get rid of the problem. It compounds it until you get a world shortage or something. The way that we did it was, to my mind, much more efficient and it was better for everybody and the person actually picking up the tab for it, the tax payer, the consumer, actually had the benefit of it. So what was wrong with that? It wasn't broke. Why did we change it?

Ian Lawton, livestock auctioneer

Forms

I do remember my uncle who was dad's boss, I called him my Uncle Bill. I do remember him filling a lot of forms in and having to colour in the colour of cattle in the official paperwork. Whether it was to do with breeding records I don't know but I remember him colouring in black and white the different – I think they were Friesians – cattle. I remember that, I'd not really thought about that for years, but he used to be filling in all this paperwork, which for a kid was sort of noticeable because they were basically pictures of animals – and for some reason, I don't know or quite understand why he did that but I think it may have been to do with breeding records.

Michael Pearson, farmer's son

Pooling Resources

We were in the early stages of our problem with Brucellosis, which causes contagious abortion in cattle. If you have an aborted calf at seven rather than nine months you don't have milk to follow along because of the lack of the stimulus of the full-term calf. Staffordshire and Derbyshire were the last to go free of Brucellosis, so there was a scheme and an incentive for us. So we went out of milk. We'd had a farm suitable for grain production and we altered the labour force because a dairyman was retiring and another lad wanted to do something else. We farmed it then as a family co-operative. Well, I say a co-operative, I mean a partnership. This entailed expanding into some contract work with the larger machinery which we needed, like a combine harvester. Forage harvesting was also a specialist machine and we did some contracting with that. It all helped improve the total income for the farm.

We would go with the machine because it would need a specialist tractor to be with it. We'd do the work along with the labour force on the farm and they'd supply some trailers. Together we would get the work done more quickly and it would help the quality of the forage that was being ensiled. Through the National Farmer's Union there was a scheme which meant you could borrow money at a relatively lower rate than the bank and through having a group of farmers, they could share that machinery and that was very helpful.

Tony Kemish, farmer

Swing of the Pendulum

I think farmers are in general much more environmentally aware than they used to be, because we are very subject to politics – and we were told to produce food and we were told to go for yield, we were told to rip out hedges, we were told to worm the animals hard, give them lots of wormer because that will keep the worms down so that they grow faster – without really realising the implications. And I think for a start, the pendulum, it's swung too far, it's swung the other way now, probably too far the other way now, but as farmers we are much more aware of any damage that we might be creating, and much less inclined to do it, even though the government tells us to.

Sue Jackson, farmer

The pendulum swings – grants for Countryside Stewardship and environmental management, 2008 © Damian Hughes

Farming and Conservation

I left college thirteen, fourteen years ago and even in my short time it's changed quite dramatically. When I first started, conservation was planting a few trees or fencing off a field corner or putting a pond in, whereas now that's completely changed. It's much more mainstream as part of the farming business with changes in policy and one thing and another. If we are talking livestock, farmers would get a subsidy from government based on the headage of stock – if you had a hundred cows as opposed to fifty cows you were getting double the subsidy. The problem with that from a conservation and land management point of view was obviously intensification – more stock means more grazing which means more fertilizer needing to be put on the land to grow more grass, then you are creating more muck which has got to go somewhere and its just an intensified system which can have a major detrimental effect on wildlife and the landscape in general. The new regime that's been brought in tries to cut the link between headage and payments so now the payment's for how many acres you farm, irrespective of whether you've got fifty or a hundred cows.

Russell Ashfield, National Trust

Hartington Cheese Factory

Origins

The original blue cheese was a complete accident. On farms they tended to keep the cheeses in the cellar to mature it on. One day somebody went down the cellar and cut a cheese open and it was mouldy. A brave soul ate it and it actually tasted quite good. Let's face it, you wouldn't make a cheese deliberately mouldy, even a hundred years ago. So what they did originally was put the mouldy cheese next to white ones and if they went blue, they were blue and if they stayed white – they stayed white. Very technical! Nowadays we help it along a bit. We add mould spores to the milk at the start of the process. But originally it was just a complete and utter accident.

The Old Cheese Shop, Hartington, 2008
© Julia Cook

Hartington Cheese Factory is famous for Stilton cheese which it's been making since 1900. It's the oldest cheese factory in the UK that's still running. It was helped by the Duke of Devonshire who around 1875 owned most of Hartington along with most of North Derbyshire and bits of Staffordshire. The Duke set it up to help his tenant farmers get rid of milk. They were getting better at making milk but having more trouble selling it. You've got to remember in 1875 Hartington was a little bit isolated. You couldn't just sort of put milk on a lorry and send it down to London or Manchester. So what you tended to make was cheese. Originally it would make

Cheshire and Derby cheese and it went fairly well for about twenty years. There were loads of cheese factories in Derbyshire, not just at Hartington.

It takes eight pints of milk to make one pound of cheese. The basic process is exactly the same as it was six thousand years ago when they first discovered it, you just use different materials to make it in. Instead of a wooden vat lined with lead or a big brass or copper kettle, now they are stainless steel vats holding thousands of litres.

A lot of cheese factories closed in 1895 because of competition from Canada, Australia, New Zealand and America and also something else had changed – the industrial revolution. We're slap bang in the middle of this sort of cheese triangle of factories, with Manchester, Sheffield, Chesterfield, Nottingham, Derby and Birmingham not so far away. These bigger towns meant there were more population and one of the things they wanted was milk, so the crop changed from cheese to milk. Instead of making cheese, farmers were selling their milk – all liquid milk to be drunk. The roads and railways opened up and now you could get rid of the milk, whereas fifty years earlier, you were isolated. It was great for the farmers at the time but not good for the cheese makers because they couldn't compete with the prices. So most of the factories closed. One by one, until only one was left – Hartington, because it makes Stilton, that's what saved it. It had a very good reputation and sold all over the country. If Hartington hadn't have been making Stilton, it wouldn't be there, it's as simple as that. I owe a lot to a bit of mouldy cheese.

Around here I've read it was called "white meat" because if you had a cow and ate it as meat, that was a one-way trip, but if you milked it you could keep making cheese which has the same nutritional value but you get more of it over the life of the animal. So it was called white meat and it was the crop.

You've heard the expression "He's the Big Cheese" or "The Big Wheel." Well that came about because if you were rich you could buy a whole wheel of cheese. If you saw someone with a whole cheese and he'd bought it from a shop or from the farm more likely, you'd say, "Well, look at him – he's the big cheese." There's another one from Leicestershire, not sure of the exact words "Drink a pot of ale a day and a scoop of Stilton and you'll live to a long age." It's supposed to be good for you, that's what they claim. And there's a saying in Melton Mowbray, "Except for the fact that they don't cry – Stilton's be more trouble than bairns..." I like that one.

Alan Salt, Hartington Cheese Factory

Peak District Dairy Wagon

Yeah, the Peak District Dairy Wagon, do you know about that? Right, that's a co-operative of dairy farmers who've got together and acquired funding to have a mobile dairy, that's just, that's very recently been launched. And you'll see it on the road shortly, and when you've seen it you'll see it, it's big, and it's got Peak District Dairy Wagon written all over it, and it's a mobile dairy that's going round the farms, participating farms, as a training device, so it comes onto a farm and teaches the farmer or whoever to make cheese, yoghurt, whatever they're going to do. It's around for a couple of years as a training device; whether it'll stay ultimately as a manufacturing unit we don't know yet. But at the moment it's a training thing, so in other words it's teaching the skills that we shouldn't have lost, to try and add value to milk, because the milk, milk farming is so dire at the moment.

Sue Jackson, farmer

16 Peak District Dairy Wagon, 2008 © Patrick Downie

16 A modern dairy unit, Peak District Dairy, Heathy Grange, Tideswell, 2008 © Damian Hughes

Beekeeper

Most people get confused. When they think of bees, they think of bumble bees which don't produce honey at all. The bees we keep look a little bit more like poorly coloured wasps, not quite so black and yellow like wasps, more a sort of brown and goldy colour. During the main part of the season the workers live for about six weeks, the queen bee can live for up to five or six years. But bees born in September will actually live until the following spring because the Queen stops laying.

It used to be that every farmer would keep bees...they were very, very common and then in the 1950s there was a disease which was called Isle of Wight disease simply because that's where it originated. It decimated the bee population so a lot of people didn't really bother after that. Suddenly honey was imported and it was easier to buy. Then individuals started up as a hobby and it's gradually building up.

We started about 15 years ago, just keeping a couple of hives in the garden, then I branched out with a couple more hives which I kept at a local farm and started from there. It's a very timeless sort of job. That's what I enjoy most. We don't use much in the way of mechanization; it's a traditional way of working and quite peaceful when you're out there with the bees working away. You have to be calm. In fact the times I get stung most is when I'm out stressed and rushing, because they feel it.

Another beekeeper said an interesting thing to me once. "What's the best thing about keeping bees?" he asked. Well, I said, "The best thing about bees must be the honey." I replied. "If it wasn't for the honey, I wouldn't keep them."

"No, the best thing about bees is that they sting."

"How do you work that out?"

"Because if bees didn't sting, everybody would keep them and you wouldn't have a business."

And I thought, yes, that's a fair point because they're brilliant, bees are brilliant.

With regards to the life cycle of a jar of honey, the bees go out from the hive and collect nectar which is basically 80% water. They bring that back to the hive and at night they all stay inside and they warm up the hive. This evaporates the water and when it's reduced down to about 20% they'll put in the honeycomb, they'll put a wax cap over it and that's the honey made. Then we use a process to remove the bees from the honey – just a simple one-way door; once they leave the honey they can't get back – that takes about 24 hours. We bring it back here, take off the capping they've put on to expose the honey, put it into a centrifuge and spin it. Then we then run it through a filter straight into jars. As simple as that.

We do warm it up very very slightly to about 16 or 17 degrees just to make it run a bit quicker. Being quite a viscous product, if we tried to bottle it at room temperature, it would take forever. It doesn't kill off any of the pollens or free radicals – the honey is still as it was intended. In a year we'll collect about 120 pounds of honey from the hives we keep at permanent sites. They need about 70 pounds themselves just to live through, so each hive on the permanent site produces about 50 pounds of honey. That cycle takes from about the beginning of April till the end of August so we're talking about five months, that's about ten pounds a month on average and in each colony, there are about 50,000 bees.

We run about 120 hives in total – 6,000,000 bees – and we keep two completely separate sets of hives. One set we keep in permanent locations around the Peak District. The other set we actually move around. At the moment we've got them on oil-seed rape and we move them over to Lincolnshire to be on borage and then we move them back on to the heather, so we actually get some of the cash crops from them. In the spring all over the Peak District we get a glut of dandelions, so the predominant flavouring in the honey now will probably be dandelions. Some areas will have more sycamore or lime in it or hawthorn so we just take what we can get basically.

Last year we took all the bees across to Lincolnshire. Most of the moving of bees is at night and we went to collect all the honey in the daytime. If you imagine each box weighs about 25 or 30 pounds and the site wasn't very close to the road. I was carrying about 50 or 60 of these boxes across the field, with bees swarming around you have to wear the whole suit and it was about 27/28 degrees centigrade. Hot, horrible, uncomfortable, heavy, hard work.

We get quite a lot of support from DEFRA. There's a regional bee inspector and because there are not many bee farmers, they actually do come out and because it's a nice area, it's a day out for them so they come out once a year and that's quite helpful.

It's a funny sort of farming; we're not bogged down by paperwork. There's none of this tagging or anything. We've got the ordinary paperwork like the Inland Revenue, VAT and that sort of stuff and doing your accounts but in terms of additional paperwork that other farmers have for keeping a record of their livestock, we don't have to do any of that.

We used to do a lot of farmers' markets and we still do, but not as many. Now we sell to gift shops and some food shops throughout the Peak District. I would say that most of our honey is actually sold not as food, but as a gift to people visiting the Peak District.

Mark Dennison, beekeeper

Shepherd

My first memory was of my mother and father working on the farm. My dad was a full-time shepherd on an estate at Edale. He was just a paid member – he didn't own any sheep. His daily duties, really, were looking after the sheep all through the year, because you started in lambing time, which is the hardest time of year, and you go on to keep the lambs alive, and there's shearing time. All these sheep live on the moors so they have to be gathered off the moors and taken back home to do everything with, so you needed dogs for that, and then the lambs go to be sold at market.

17 Geoff Townsend, Shepherd, 2008 © Peter Miles

I used to love lambing time because my dad used to walk everywhere, he used to go around with his flock of sheep, he had eight hundred ewes and he used to walk round five times a day. He would start at half past five in the morning and not back until about midnight and so, of course, we used to have our breakfast – if we were at school we might go in the morning and help before school – just have a walk around and you are learning all the time at that age. If we were at school we would go to school and come back home and have our tea and then we would go for a bit of a play somewhere and then we might go up and feed some lambs.

Sheep Shearing

The animals are sheared normally towards the end of June and beginning of July, depending on the weather. You have to go the right way round a sheep because it helps your back and you have to move the sheep around you, rather than you move around the sheep. And you have to try to get as close to the skin as you can so you are getting the most wool off, and you have to make it nice and clean so that you don't cut into the wool. It's called double cutting where you cut the wool in half – it cuts the fibre in half so it makes it less valuable – it's harder to spin it that way. You've got to keep the shearing head close to the sheep at all times so as to get a nice clean cut and keep the fleece in one piece. On my dad's farm the next door neighbours would come and help my dad shear and he would go and help them shear the next week. Farmers used to help each other shear the sheep. When I was young, everyone sheared their own sheep, but now it's all contractors. It's totally changed. I'm a contract shepherd, so I don't own any sheep either, I work for different people – I'm self-employed.

18 Sheep-shearing. George and William Gregory, Blackwell Hall Farm c.1930s
© Courtesy of Angela Taylor, from the Gregory Collection

The Year

Lowland flocks will lamb around the middle of March but your main hill flocks will lamb around about the tenth of April. It usually takes around six weeks to lamb a flock of sheep. So you've done the lambing and tried to make every lamb live, and they all want castrating or their tails taken off, probably ear marking and a little colour tag on them to show who they belong to. If the sheep are off the moors they go back onto the moors with their lambs and the poorly sheep stay back to be looked after – all the healthy ones are on the hills. You get a bit of a break then. You could probably do a couple of jobs around the farm for a fortnight or three weeks and then shearing time will appear at the end of June so then all the sheep have to be gathered back in off the moors which is probably two or three days job just to collect them all in. They'll all obviously be sheared and need marking and probably a dose of wormer, looking at to make sure their feet are okay and the lambs will probably get a wormer and a health check as well. Then they all go back on the moors again. Next it's dipping time so they have to come back off the moors again, go in the tub, dipped for the parasites on their skin, another health check probably and back on the moors. Around about the first week in October they come back down and all the lambs will stay at home to be sorted out for market. All the lambs are sorted into grades; some might go straight for meat and some are what they call store lambs, which you take to market and people buy to fatten on. The ewes go back on the hill on their own and they call that flushing the ewes. The lambs are not there anymore and the ewes won't go to ram until the end of November so they have a period without where they can get themselves a bit better and put some flesh on their bones.

19 Andrew Boam, farmer – feeding sheep, Longnor, 2008 © Julia Cook

After that they'll be fed every day with hay and then they'll go back on the moors about the second week in January. By that time most of the lambs should've gone but there's always a bit of dog training to do and dry stone walling, maintenance that sort of stuff, a bit of fencing, there's always some jobs at the farm to do. At the end of March the sheep come back a fortnight before they lamb just so they are not running around too hard when they are heavy in lamb, they're all settled down at home, and then you start the process again.

Geoffrey Townsend, shepherd

Pet Lambs

We had a pet sheep, she'd had lambs. She couldn't feed both, so one was brought up on the bottle. In years to come she had lambs herself but what did she do? She wouldn't stop with the other sheep. She used to come and bring them to the house door.

"These are my lambs. You feed them."

She would do it regularly but once I'd spoken to them.....

20 Bottle-fed lambs, Over Haddon, 2003 © Jake Mycock

We'd one that was blind. It couldn't help itself so I fed it and it lived so long in the kitchen till it had to go outside and the children took over bottling her. They used to tease her. She got as she knew where things were, the corn store. And the yard was on a slope and you could go two ways to the house, down the yard or through the plantation. They'd go both ways to try and lose her. But she got wise to them. They'd set off one way and she'd go the other and she could find her way although she was blind.

She knew exactly what she was doing. If the doors of the corn store weren't open, sliding doors, she would rub first one way and then the other and if the catch hadn't been put on they would slide and she could get in and help herself and gorge on the corn. And she got two red sides because the oil out of her fleece rubbed on the red of the corn store door. There was another sheep that pined. We took her over to the other ground because we didn't want her near the house. 'She'd been out about a week and Brian said, "I'm going to have to bring Susie home, she's losing herself." She went fat but she wasn't going to a local butcher or else. I said, "I'm not having that back as a piece of meat." I wasn't one of those that could eat something that I'd reared. It'd be like eating my friend. No, I was a bit sentimental like that. I know a lot of people say there's nothing nicer than something you've fed but, no, I couldn't.

Margaret Oven, farmer's wife

Sheep's Milk

I milk sheep, Dorset sheep, because they'll lamb at different times of the year, because a sheep does not have a long lactation, very short compared with a cow. They're all home bred. I've been a closed flock since about 1990, something like that. For health reasons primarily, and also in my job, because I want to milk them, a sheep if it doesn't want to be milked can be really quite difficult. It will be very disruptive because with sheep if somebody panics everybody panics, and then you've got a real mess on your hands, so it's easier to have home-bred ones, because I know what I'm dealing with. They milk very quickly, in about two minutes, unlike a cow which takes a lot longer,

It's much richer. It's much higher in fat, it's higher in total solids, it's about double, so if you're making a sheep cheese out of it, the yield of cheese will be twice what it would be out of cow's milk, it's so concentrated, basically. You can make anything out of it, although it doesn't work very well with butter, because the cream doesn't rise to the top, but anything else, just the same. I freeze it. It freezes and it's just like normal milk, so on a day-to-day basis I freeze it, and I do have a certain amount of fresh milk customers, and sell a certain amount on farmers' markets, but I could produce and turn more over if it was made into something, into yoghurt or cheese, which I'll do on the Dairy Wagon.

Sue Jackson, farmer

21 Sue and Erica Jackson sheep-milking, 2008 © Damian Hughes

Bulls

He used to always have a big bull Mr Burnet did, and you always had to watch 'im. When I was working at Clem Simpson's – he reared them short-horned bulls. They were only about this bloomin' big but I always kept boss 'cause we used to have to take 'em out to water every morning and I always took a stick with me and he always played backing – go down the field backwards – and I used to clout him with a stick. I kept the boss of him. One day I was helping some builders do a shed roof and Clem had gone down to village to shop, and he were coming back and we heard this voice shouting "Help! Help!" This little bull had got him down on the ground and he'd got hold of his nose. He'd started playing with him, backing back and eventually he just bumped into his legs and knocked him down. I ran down the field to him and when this bull saw me coming he were off, because he was always frightened of me. He'd have mauled him if we hadn't have heard this shouting from the building roof. After that we got him in and put a ring in his nose.

Bill Chadwick, farmer

Breaking In Horses

It was all horses in my grandfather's day. There was not a tractor in the valley. He had seventeen brood mares, so he had seventeen foals every year and then he bought in younger foals and would break them in to harness. There's quite an art you know. If you had a bad tempered one, it wasn't worth having, they could kill somebody and did. The young horses were sent up to the limestone above Castleton there for the summer, to grow the bone in them from yearlings up to two year olds. Of course they weren't broken in to shaft until they were three years old, two years in their traces. There were four sons at home but he had a hundred acres of arable and a quarter of it was bare fallow, for two reasons. It cleaned the ground of weeds and it found work for these young horses in the summer time, because unless you kept them at work they got out of hand. They used to say they broke the collar. They used to tell us such stories about breaking these horses...They would get a gang of them, all the local lads and they would ride, of course, bare-back, this horse and they would jump off and another jump on and they'd go again and go again until they'd exhausted it and then they'd put a collar on it. The first thing they did was to gradually bring it to pulling things. They'd graduate then to a roller. Grandfather told a story about a roller and this young horse. They hit something and made a rattle and it

22 Farming with horse power. Arthur Ollerenshaw, Grindlow, 1930s
Unknown. © Courtesy The Ollerenshaw Family

bolted and jumped a fence with the horse on one side and roller on the other. They had problems of getting it off, of course.

Everything in those days was horses. I can remember going to Sheffield because at that time you only kept one horse because one horse ate as much as two cows, but many times we wanted a second horse in the summer to get the crops in and you could buy one out of the town that had been on the hard road such a long time that its legs had gone, not badly but it had problems with its fetlocks and it wanted to go on soft ground. So you could buy one, probably for £20. I remember going with my father and a neighbour of his to this huge stable in Sheffield where the City Corporation kept its horses. There must have been eighty horses back to back.

Ray Platts, farmer

Ploughing

It was alright as long as you didn't get in a field where you'd got some rock and then you'd got to watch your ribs. If you were steering it and hit a lump of rock it'd knock the plough out and it can knock you over. Two handles to steer the plough and the two horses pulling it.

Bill Chadwick, farmer

23 Horse-drawn plough. Arthur Ollerenshaw, Grindlow, 1930s
Unknown. © Courtesy The Ollerenshaw Family

Making Hay

We'd all the Spring work to do: chain farrowing and muck spreading and building gaps up till Summer came along. We didn't have a tractor, just two horses. I did all the horse work with a two-horse mowing machine. Sometimes I could ride on the back if I felt a bit tired. A lot of it was leading them by the bridles. We swaft-turned[2] and hay-raked with a horse rake. In them days you had to pitch it with a fork and you put it into two big rows and you went up between with a cart. You'd two throwing it up at you off the floor with two forks, big forkfuls. You'd got to straighten it out and had to build it up on the wagon or cart – what we called a 'raise' in them days. On each corner you'd put a stick and you had to start building from your corners. Each corner then one in the middle and carry on up your load until you got to the front and put it on again – one on each corner – keep your middle full they always said. You'd got a man on each side picking it up and one on the load, loading it as loose hay. It was really hard work, especially with the very hot weather we used to have in them days.

---

2 Derbyshire for swath or swathe, a line of grass, cereal or similar crops left after scything, mowing or reaping.

24 Hay Harvest c.1930s © Courtesy Bill Chadwick and REAP

Mostly it was stored in barns. Ones you could get inside so you didn't have to turn out in winter for it - without hay you couldn't keep the cattle over winter. We made a couple of big stacks sometimes out in' fields - same as stacking it on the loader. Always keep your middle well full and it sort of drains off more right from the top then. If you've got your middle going down, water runs into the stack, not out. We started building it and going in gradually till it come to a point like. Then after that we just had to go around and pull off all the loose stuff. We'd probably get half a cart load to pull off and then we'd have to stack up with that again and then they'd just have to thatch them. I remember going up to Winkhill. They used to grow a lot of rushes up there and we'd just fetch loads for thatching. About the same as a thatched cottage today. Thatching strings and pegs... we just had to get pegs out of the nut-wood ... you get them about that long... with a point on..... and then you pushed them in the stack. You didn't push them down, you pushed them more or less upwards so it didn't encourage water to go in then. It was quite a work of art, farming was in them days.

Bill Chadwick, farmer

25 On the silage clamp today, Heathy Farm, Tideswell, 2008 © Damian Hughes

Harvesting

They could do it very quickly and that was a sheaf you see and that had to be set up. You had ten sheaves in what we called a kiver in these parts, some parts call them stooks, and that consisted of two sheaves there and three at each side and two on top upside down so they were safe from the rain and the birds. They said you had to let the church bells ring twice on the corn - they had to stay out two weeks to finish drying, then you could harvest it - that was always September.

The corn was made into stacks, little round ones. You've quite a small base and then it came out right up to the base of the roof so that the water didn't run onto the straw. It's quite a skill building them – the farm workers built them. I've seen thirty or forty around the farm. My father used to thatch them, it wasn't the same as thatching houses. Straw for thatching wasn't grown at home; it was delivered in what they called bottles, great big straw sheaves that had been thrashed just on the ends. They didn't put the whole thing through the thrasher, they'd have broken the straw. On wet days, they would 'draw the thatch.' Comb it, so all the bits of leaves and rubbish were removed so you were left with lovely straight pieces of straw. Then you put thatch on, you drove thatch pegs through them and took this – what you call welching - rot-proof very coarse rope and it went round the thatch pegs and on to the next one to hold it on. And then the next layer came over until you were up to the top. They used to be very particular about thatching. It was all trimmed off at the bottom right round up to the top and they'd have a corn dolly or something right on the top. They were fertility symbols, symbols for the harvest.

Bill Gregory, farmer

Threshing

One early recollection is threshing. We probably grew about thirty acres of cereals which we cut with a binder and stacked. Then the thresher, Mr Morgan, would come in February with his steam engine named Dolly. It was mine and my sister's job to cart the chaff away from the thresher and that was really dirty. We started dead on eight o'clock, didn't stop until eleven for a cup of tea and went

26 Feeding a steam-powered threshing machine. Undated.
© Courtesy Angela Taylor, origin unknown

on until about one o'clock. In those days we had about six or eight people came to help us. It's a full time job when you're threshing, you've got probably three people on the stacks, one forking the sheaves to another who cut the bands on the sheaves and then a third feeding the drum, and then I suppose we got between three-quarters and a ton an hour out of it and that was all used for home consumption. We may have sold some of the wheat but we grew mainly oats in those days, not much wheat and very little barley but when the war took over we had to grow wheat which the Government bought off us. Bread was never rationed during the war, it wasn't rationed until 1952. We had the first combine in 1961 and of course that transformed the job altogether.

James Furness, farmer

Crops

Well, they always said Cow Close was a little bit of Lincolnshire dropped into Derbyshire. Because they had some flat fields at the bottom and they were long, all in a long line, from up at the top where the woods stopped, all the way down until the bottom. And those fields were lovely and flat, and they grew corn. Which very few people grew round here. It wasn't corn growing country. But they always had nice crops down there, and potatoes, and turnips, there wasn't much choice, it was a milking farm.

Jean Brocklehurst, farmer's wife

27 Planting potatoes in Thomas Maltby's field, c. 1950s © Len Furness, courtesy John Furness

Peak Ales Brewery

Peak Ales is a ten barrel plant and a barrel is thirty-six gallons so we produce 360 gallons at a time and we brew twice a week. It takes the best part of a day before the yeast will go in and it will probably take between three and five days to bring the gravity down at which stage we'll put some cooling on and slow the process right down and give it a couple of days of cooling and then we'll transfer it into conditioning tanks where it'll have another couple of days conditioning and then we'll look to put it into casks and send it out to trade.

Primarily our customers are the local free trade. It's been very rewarding to see your beer available in the Peak District when you go out and we've had great support from the local free trade. We are part of a scheme by SIBA – the Society of Independent Brewers. They set up a scheme called Enterprise Inns whereby we can do a direct delivery with them. So we deliver to their free trade outlets, as they call them, for a local beer, if the landlord requests. Of course he has to buy it through Enterprise but we deliver it directly and that's helped as well. That's a good access to market for us.

Small breweries, I think, will develop. I think people are looking for a more local product that is green in its outlook which they can relate to. There's every

28 Rob Evans testing the liquor temperature, 2007 © Photo: Ken Davis

chance the route to market will improve. I would like to think so. That's our only concern. There's certainly sufficient customer demand, it's just that quite a lot of the public houses are either tied to a brewery or the like who have got quite strong buying power and aren't as flexible in allowing the landlords to have what they would particularly like to sell. But there's a groundswell of public opinion that would want micro-breweries to be available, to be local. It's just making sure we've got the access to market.

It's a family-run business and my father was instrumental and integral to the start of the brewery. About a year ago we took on Stuart and that's let my dad off with a little less work but as time's gone by, we've brewed more so there's been more jobs to do and that's how I'd like to see it going – nice and steadily but going a little bit bigger. It is a commercial enterprise and it's got to pay its way. Long term? I'd just like to see us growing nicely so that we're representative of the Peak District and people. If they know about the Peak District they'll associate us with it from a brewing point of view.

I think it's always nice to locate yourself so that's why Bakewell Best Bitter was chosen. And we do a winter warmer, 'Noggin Filler'. I just liked the sound of that and having looked up that a Noggin was associated with alcoholic drinks – I thought, well that's good enough for me. When it comes to naming the beers, it's a job really that we all contribute to but I think I have the final decision. We always wanted it to reflect the locality or deal with something on a local theme. Swift Nick, our 3.8 session ale was given the name because I was looking for a local character and I was reading a book called *Dick Turpin in Derbyshire* and it detailed the story of this gentleman highwayman, Swift Nick robbing a farmer on his way home from Bakewell market. So I thought that's good enough local provenance and I liked the name Swift Nick. When people have asked you "Oh, are you going to have a drink?" you might reply "I'll just have a swift one."

Rob Evans, Peak Ales Brewery

Wagon Wheels

If you wanted a new cart or a new wagon or anything it was made at the local joiners down the road and then it went up' the blacksmith at Hope to have the steel put round the wheels, which was an art in itself. They had to be bent from cold, they had to be made exactly the right size to be put on and when they were joined they had to be overlapped and then hammered together in hot steel – there was no welding in those days. When they finally came to putting them on the wheels, they needed about four young fellas to work the blower on the fire and you weren't paid for this, they just asked your father if they could borrow you for a day and that were it.

It was nice to get off the farm, get a bit of company and chat, that sort of thing,

29 Cartwheel hoops at the Georgian Forge, Blackwell, 2008 © Damian Hughes

but I always remember the grandfather, he sat on a large log and he had an ash stick. If you blew too hard you got a welt across your back with it because you blew the fire right out you see, and if you didn't blow hard enough you got one across your legs, so you knew which was which. They turned this huge wheel through the fire, kept turning and turning and turning until it was really hot and then rushed outside and put it on this wooden wheel and then threw water on it to expand the wood and of course in the summertime that's what you had to do, keep wetting them because otherwise the rim would come off.

Ray Platts, farmer

Worthy of Hire

You know the old saying "working for relationships is the worse ship that ever sailed." It was my mother's auntie, that was. Ooh she did keep you going. She had a lot of hens and then I had to go and feed them and collect eggs, clean them out while she used to go upstairs and watch me go around. It was all flat ground and she could see all the hencotes and if I were in a bit longer than I should have been she asked, "What are you doin' in there?" We had four or five big cotes – a lot of eggs. I was fifteen, going to sixteen. 'Were there twelve months and I got twelve pounds plus food. Pound a month or about seven pence a day.

30 Modern hencotes, Heathy Grange, Tideswell, 2008 © Damian Hughes

A fella named Clement Simpson at May Furlong offered me twenty five pounds for twelve months and I thought that was a big increase. Mind you it was a good place too – a good table and everything and you didn't get worked... you put your hours in and that, so I stopped there four years till just after the war started. I had to go in the army otherwise, so I went to Mr Burnet's at Buck Furlong again at Grindon after that. We just had a holiday at Christmas – what they called Hiring Fayre for farm workers. It used to go to Leek Market and I never did go there but you just go to Leek and you bargain for a wage for the twelve months and if they agreed they gave them a shilling and that shilling fastened them. They couldn't go to anybody else. You could choose where you went to, and if you were a good worker you didn't have to go to the hiring fayre really. When I left Leek, Clem – I always called him Clem – Clem Simpson found out I was coming and he came down and asked me direct.

Bill Chadwick, farmer

A fourteen day week

My father said he wasn't going to milk again if he bought a milking machine, and he never milked again after that, so I'd always got it to do, night and morning, twice a day, day in, day out. It's a fourteen day week. Today there's so many farmers going out of milk because of the labour. They've either got to do it themselves, or pay for labour. I was at a meeting recently and they were saying that the price of wheat in 1840 would, per ton, employ a farm man then for a hundred and forty days. Today it'll pay for two days. The values and prices have changed, and it's the same with farm wages, and milk. Nobody can make a living with under a hundred cows now, and if you've overheads, and expense, like labour... No wonder they're all going out of milk. Even the Queen's sold her Ayrshire herd. If she can't make it pay, there's not much chance for anybody else.

Thomas Maltby, farmer

The Cow Club

I was a part-time farmer really, worked on the railways, British Rail, but as an adult farmer I was responsible for about thirty cows. The Cow Club started in 1838. It was a local club really. They were small farmers, all small farmers, like me. Anybody could join it. Insurance for cattle, against cattle diseases.

Every cow had to be kept within a mile and a half of Tideswell Church. It was in the rule book that. About 1964 I was made the secretary and was involved in the club for about forty years. You had to pay so much a month, every three months. For the start, you had to pay to join, and then it was so much a year and then for five years and then it dropped down to four shillings a year. If a cow died, the club paid for it. About eleven pound in about 1940. Yes, it was quite a good organisation.

Though we now only keep sheep, I've been a member of the Cow Club since I was seventeen and I'm still a member. They have a supper every year, you know and that's the main part. We have had things like trips around to look at other farms and things like that, but they don't do so much now. It's mainly a social thing.

Wilf Oven, farmer

31 Cow Club Dinner, c.1982 © Courtesy Harold Oven

The High Peak Livestock Society

It was formed with twelve farmers in 1974 at a meeting in The Cat and Fiddle. To be a member you couldn't be a dealer and you had to receive hill farm subsidy.

It was absolutely unique. We were their auctioneers, and at their first sale I think we had four hundred and twenty odd cattle and it's blossomed to what it is today. They have a dozen sales or more a year of sheep and cattle. They're conducted in Bakewell now but then they were out on field sites, the sheep sales were.

Ian Lawton, livestock auctioneer

The Slaughterman's Art

Yesterday

Hathersage had a slaughterhouse, at the junction on the left hand side where the butcher's shop and the car park is. That's where they slaughtered them, where the car park is now. It was open to the village and I can remember a lad from school. He'd gone for his apprenticeship there. In those days they pole-axed them. A pole-axe was like a pick only it had a very sharp probe, you know sharpened to a point – you just drove it in to the back of the head. Go in about six inches – straight through the brain. A good man would do it, but he was nervous I suppose. They got this animal tied down to a ring and he knocked both horns off while he was trying to pole-axe him, he was bellowing away... I don't know what they'd think about those things today but eventually somebody killed it.

The chappie that used to do the slaughtering would take bets that he could kill, skin and dress a lamb while the church clock struck twelve and he'd always get his lunch that way. Mind you it was a liquid lunch, but he always got his lunch that way. It's amazing when you tell people today, they think it can't be done, but he could do it.

Ray Platts, farmer

Today

When I was young, which wasn't that long ago, every village had its own little slaughterhouse and all the animals were taken there. There was no stress involved – you could even walk them there. If an animal gets really stressed, the blood sugar levels get high and the meat will cut very dark. That accelerates the maturation period and the meat, especially vacuum-packed, will not keep. There's no detriment to the eating of it but it will not keep because it's had that stress.

Years ago in a slaughterhouse, a man would dress each individual animal himself. Dressing an animal means basically taking the skin or the hide off it. A proper skilled slaughterman can do the whole job. The old slaughterhouses never used to touch the animal with anything other than a knife and you might have a cloth if you dared get any dirt on the carcass. A real slaughterman takes real pride in his job.

The modern slaughterhouses have what they call a line system. One man will shoot it. One man will take the skin off the leg. Another will take the skin off down off the side of the ribs. So it's a line system, like working in a car factory really. They've got these hose pipes and they're swilling them up and down but there's a membrane between the meat and the hide which people aren't aware of. It's not visible with the naked eye. And when they do the hosing down, that gets rid of that membrane and that is another factor in the keeping of the meat. It doesn't keep as long. It's a real skill to slaughter an animal but now there's no skill, its just throughput. The industry is short of skilled men who can do the job from "the gate to the plate."

Mick Shirt, master butcher

Mushroom Growth

My grandfather sold crops into Sheffield because they needed a large amount of fodder for these horses that were in town and he sold hay into Sheffield and brought manure back. My father told a story about getting up one morning and he thought it had snowed and it was mushrooms and they said they only picked the best but they sent four cartloads into Sheffield and that was because of the manure that had come out of Sheffield. There's nothing like horse manure for growing mushrooms.

Ray Platts, farmer

Blown

If an animal was blown, bicarbonate of soda was one that we used to give. Blown, well, pot bellied, they fill up with gas, perhaps overeating, gorged on grass. With a big animal you've got to be quick. Sticking it, wasn't it called? A cannula I think, that you put in. It's almost like a sharp point. A needle would do it to puncture. But you've got to keep the hole open and the gases puff out. But this had a centre in it. You puncture it and pull the centre out. Every farmer had a penknife, pocket knife I should say. It's a case of don't leave it too long. If it was bad you would deal with it rather than lose it. We saved quite a few animals through doing it. You keep your eye on them and take them away from the source if you can do. But, quite often, when you find an animal it's down and so you've got to deal with it.

Margaret Oven, farmer's wife

Foot and Mouth

Any surplus cattle we had we didn't take to market, a cattle dealer used to buy them because there was virtually no transport but he had his own cattle truck. In about 1937 Foot and Mouth struck a farm down the lane about five-hundred

32 Disinfecting for Foot and Mouth disease, Jean and Tom Brocklehurst, 1967
© Tom Brocklehurst

yards away. Fortunately it stayed down there but we had to walk past it to go to school. They put restrictions on movement of cattle, I don't know if they closed the market at Bakewell. I well remember the fire where they burned the carcases and the field where they dug a big pit and put them in. I can smell it now, it's a smell that you'll never forget. Then there was one in Castlegate in 1967. They thought it was brought on the tyres on the trucks from Cheshire which came to Glebe Mine. That was contained but it was a bit upsetting at the time because the neighbouring farmer had been on our farm the day before and they took all his cattle as well.

James Furness, farmer

There were five farms caught up in the Foot and Mouth at Edale in 1967 and everything was slaughtered. We didn't go to school for six weeks. And we had a policeman at the bottom of the lane so whenever you wanted anything you would have to write it on a bit of paper and he would go to the shop and bring it back. You couldn't move anything anywhere. They killed all the animals on the farm and burned them – there were great big trenches, it was called the House Meadow and four Irish men stayed there for about a week just shovelling coal on. I can remember my dad crying, it was an awful time.

Geoffrey Townsend, shepherd

Lead Poisoning

My husband's mother, she was in bed very ill in '63 and one morning she came out with "Don't let those hens out on to the ground"

"Why Mother?"

"Because of the belland.... You must not let those young stock go onto certain fields. Now don't forget."

This was all when she was not well. We took it that she was rambling. In later years we found out that she was not rambling, to our detriment. We lost animals.

It's something to do with the lead. There'd been lead mines, what they call mine rakes. And it brings up, it's like a blue haze on the ground with the dew, that's early in the morning, you see. Various little things like that, as I say, you think, "Oh, it can't be," but, obviously, it is. It's lead poisoning. Animals will die. You can tell really because they are not growing as they ought to do. You

33 Lead Rake, Nether Wheal, near Sheldon, 2005 © Damian Hughes

think, perhaps they are not getting enough milk, like, we'd a cow with two calves, they were twins, well, she lost them both. But they got to a point when they weren't growing as they ought. She was doing all right. But it's young stock that it poisons. And we've even lost lambs. It's in the ground. It comes up in the soil. Especially when you get moles working. They bring up the soil from underneath and, if you notice, quite often lambs will play round and suck and do, round the heaps, they'll run and paw at it to have a suck.

That was one point; you don't always take notice.

Margaret Oven, farmer's wife

Power

Someone once asked me what was the biggest advance in farming in my lifetime and I said it was the power we were given and they thought I was talking about political power. But I wasn't, I was meaning the difference between when I was a child if you couldn't do it by hand, your hands or you couldn't do it by horse, it couldn't get done and it was mostly one horse. For instance when we came here we grew a field of peas because some of the ground had had five or six crops of corn and it wouldn't grow anything else. Well, we'd no means of cutting it, only a horse-drawn mowing machine and you went up with it and you couldn't see what you had done so you had then to pull it all out, and go to the next one and pull it all out... I think it took us about five days to cut three acres.

Nowadays you'd go in with a tractor with a power-driven machine behind it and you'd do it in half an hour. And when you brought a horse home after you'd been working it, you had to wash its shoulders with salt water to get the sweat out of it otherwise you'd get a blister and it wouldn't work. Today you just turn a key in a

34 Machine power, Home Farm, Hassop 2008 © Damian Hughes

tractor; he thought I was talking about political power. Only the working day's longer, not shorter. We've got twice the acreage and half the labour force.

Ray Platts, farmer

The Application of Science

None of these things were like drawing the curtains. They evolved, like everything else. But science has brought capability. When my father was a dairy farmer, we had plenty of cows that would have eight, ten, eleven, twelve calves. In the dairy cow, when I left school in 1958, the average annual yield was about seven hundred and fifty gallons. We're now at eight or nine thousand litres, so it's gone up by a factor of three in fifty years. Yet the cow's calving lactations on average is about two and a half lactations instead of eight to twelve. It could go even less. Economics and science mean cows turn grass into milk three times as fast as they did fifty years ago, yet need replacing twice as often.

Ian Lawton, livestock auctioneer

Changes

There were more dairy farms. A lot more. It was a commonplace if you were going along a country road you'd have to wait and let the cows go past on their way to milking. It's happened to me once in I don't know how many years. Those small herds are nearly all gone. Their land's been sold off or they've gone for horses. Incomers have bought them and they're now pony paddocks.

Sue Jackson, farmer

35 Cattle on the road, Earl Sterndale 2007 © Damian Hughes

Market

How does farm-produce become food? As well as through the efforts of brewers (page 49), cheese-makers (page 31), poachers (page 81) and gamekeepers (page 83) etc, it travels through the farm gate on its way to markets and shops. It may go through this cycle two or three times. As Russell Ashfield says 'People don't realise if you want a joint of beef it's a three year process...' (page 81) where live-stock markets, for example, are a means to an end, not the end itself. Each stage should add quality or value. Care and attention is given to providing and taking the best.

In the traditional model where food travels no more than a wagon (horse or motor-powered) or train journey from source to destination in less than a day, freshness is taken for granted and the idea of a sell-by date almost nonsensical. Similarly seasonality becomes an anticipation where new potatoes or spring lamb are natural highlights rather than year-round fare. It also leaves a far smaller carbon-footprint since food miles are measured in tens not thousands.

Yet today, the traditional model is seen as something of a rarity, if not luxury. 'Old-fashioned' shops are forever disappearing, Killer's Bakery in Wirksworth (page 93) Nelsons Pork Pie Makers and Skidmores' greengrocers in Bakewell (page 70) have all gone in the last few years, together with a way of bringing and keeping local produce, producers and customers together. Farmers' Markets (page 79), Chatsworth Farm Shop (page 77), both relatively recent returns to tradition, are more for specialities rather than everyday fare. Perhaps butchers such as Mycocks of Buxton, (page 88) or Mick Shirt at Critchlows of Bakewell (page 86), who know their meat and customers equally well, satisfy both needs. Quality and reputation take time to achieve and are passed on by word of mouth. Christine Elliot's family has run the fish and chip shop in Tideswell (page 97) for over three generations, well before McDonalds started. They don't need to advertise and their renown was sufficient to gain mention in the Egon Ronay Good Food Guide.

Every third pound in the High Street is spent at Tesco, and even a community and socially focused chain such as the Co-op (page 75) stocks its shelves from an immense distance. We follow, like lambs to the slaughter. In a telling phrase of the Dowager Duchess of Devonshire, describing the travails of establishing the farm shop at Chatsworth, "so they went to Sainsbury's where lamb is for ever and knows no seasons." Seasonality is denied, instead of welcomed. Why? It seems price and speed are considered more vital than provenance and quality, even though shopping today is as much a leisure pursuit as it is a necessity.

Packaging is the most visible sign of this process, as Ray Platts (page 62) points out. Where a paper bag was once sufficient for most things, supermarket shelves are full of items that are wrapped twice or thrice-fold, all in the name of 'freshness.' It's hard now to imagine a village shop (page 68) where almost everything not in a tin was weighed and measured individually – in pounds and ounces, to be paid for in pounds, shillings and pence. Too easily bought today, too easily thrown away.

It's almost as hard to imagine things changing significantly, although initiatives such as Peak Choice (page 81) aim to bring a broader market to local producers. In this section you can appreciate how food for these people and their customers isn't something anonymous and mass-produced, where you don't know quite where it came from:

"Quality will always win through on price." Mick Shirt.

"We've got a lovely shop. Fantastic custom, fantastic people." Roy Mycock.

The Saga of the Milk Cheque – A Hard Day's Night

This tale I've told many, many times. You sent your milk to dairies, they're only small dairies. One man would probably have the milk from two or three farms and of course they were always strapped for money and didn't like to pay. This particular chap had not paid Grandfather for quite a while so Grandmother said, "You're going to have to go and see this chap, we're running very low on funds." Away he went on the train to Manchester and caught up with this man but he wouldn't talk about money. Grandfather kept on trying to broach the subject. By about ten o'clock he finally managed to get some money out of him. All the regular trains had gone so he went on the station and there was just an express for London.

He shouted up to the driver, "Any chance for stopping at Miller's Dale?"

"Have you a sovereign?"

"Yes."

"Right ye are – jump up!"

36 Miller's Dale viaduct, 2008 © Damian Hughes

He went onto the footplate and sparks flew and wheels spun and away he went, you know, like hell t'wards Miller's Dale and the driver said, "I can't stop, its more than me job's worth, I shall slow down, I shall tap you on the shoulder at Miller's Dale and you'll have to jump out." About eleven o'clock at night the driver slowed down and Grandfather jumped out in Cheedale. The sparks flew and away the train went into the night and he couldn't tell where on earth he was. It was completely dark, he hadn't got a torch or anything. It was all bridges, tunnels or steep embankments. Anyway, he slithered down the embankment, walked through the river, clawed his way up the wood and arrived home about midnight, absolutely covered in greenery and soil. That was the saga of the milk cheque – the things they had to do.

Bill Gregory, farmer

Milk Rounds

Between The Wars

I was christened Frank Raymond Platts and I've always been known as Raymond because my father was Frank, and mother said I'm not having "Young Frank" and "Old Frank," so I've always been known by my middle name. I only had one brother, who was unfortunately killed in the war. He could milk cows when he was four years old! Unfortunately I had very weak wrists and couldn't squeeze. It was all hand-milked in those days, so I got the other jobs. I had to get the sticks in, get the coal in, clean my father's shoes, wellingtons and his leggings, 'cause in those days you know we only milked twelve or fourteen cows and the milk was delivered around the village twice in the day, so you had to look smart.

We delivered it in cans, measured it out and you'd have people that would have half a pint in the

37 Collection of early milk-churns, 2008
© Lynne Mycock

morning and half a pint at night, thinking they'd get more milk, because you only carried a pint measure. You had all sorts, you had women who put a basin out or something; they'd say the cat's knocked the plate off the top and drunk it – all kinds of things to get out of paying!

It was...wait a minute, three ha'pence a pint in old money. I remember my father saying about my uncle, who'd had the farm before us. He had one woman there who never had anything there to put the milk in, you know, he had to either get a pan or a jug or something and wash it up. She would never get out of bed and he went to the bottom of the stairs and shouted "Come on, get up and get me something to put the milk in," and she said "Can't you find anything?" and he looked around till he found a colander and he put it in the middle of the table and poured the milk in. He said there was always something to put it in after that!

I was born four years after the Great War and the majority of children had no father. There was one lady in the village when I was taking milk round and she'd three teenage sons then, all in work, and she used to have three pints of milk in a jug that if you filled it within half an inch of the top there was no need to measure it. The jug wasn't there one morning, only a chamber pot on the side. I asked "What are you doing with this, Mrs Rookes?" She said "Put it in that." "Are you sure?" "Yes! Put it in that! The little buggers! Every time they go past, they pick it up and have a drink and I'm left with a little drop in' bottom to make the meal at night." She said, "I'm gonna cure them!"

Ray Platts, farmer

Today

I was born in 1957 in Glossop, Derbyshire. As a five year old we went to a little place called Birch Vale, nice little dairy farm, 42 acres, milked about 30 cows. My dad said "Well it's like this, there are plenty of chimneys, so we should be able to sell plenty of milk". We moved all the furniture and everything in a cattle wagon from Marple up to the farm in Birch Vale.

Every weekend I'd help me dad on a Saturday collecting the money and that's how I really started in the milk business. It was green top milk then, straight from the cow, not pasteurised. My dad never delivered a pint of pasteurised milk funnily enough, and he did a milk round for 58 years. It was straight from the cow, straight into the churns or the bulk tank, straight to the bottles and out on the milk round. There's no fresher milk than that.

I got married at 23 and came to live at Wardlow. We were beef and sheep farmers, and George bought a little milk round and he used to deliver in Eyam, and so I helped him when I wasn't at work and that's how I sort of started on the milk business myself. We'd got two children then and I wanted a little bit of pin money, so I said, "How about me starting a round of my own?" I put some cards through

38 Pauline Jackson and her milk van, 2008 © Hannah Watson

the door and I got seven replies. So I went with the seven. We've since had another son, and from seven, I've four hundred customers. I still love every single minute of it. I get up at two thirty in the morning and then I'm with the van for about three o'clock. I'm very lucky, my carbon footprint is nil because I don't travel to work. My first customer is my next door neighbour and I start in the village that I live in, Sheldon, and I deliver down through Sheldon and pick a load of milk up from Ashford-in-the-Water. I deliver round Ashford and Great Longstone and I go and pick the second load up and go down into Bakewell because it's a very, very big tourist area. So I do all my households first and then go to the cafés and pubs. I'm finished for about ten o'clock in the morning, so I do alright.

I decided to go on to glass bottles, because I do think that that is recycling and re-usability to the hilt. The foil top can be re-used as well, that can be recycled. I even take people's back to have them recycled with the Scouts and Guides of Bakewell, so every way round, it's a wonderful service. I saw a chap one day, gets in his Jaguar, goes down to the shop and buys a pint of milk and comes back up, seven o'clock in the morning. I'm there with the van outside his house, milk on board...talk about carbon footprint...the money that he wasted and the petrol going down to the shop was more than what he'd have paid to me. Milk tastes and keeps better in glass bottles too.

My father gave me a lot of confidence, in that if you provide a good service,

39 Modern glass milk bottles, already almost antique, 2008 © Lynne Mycock

that's what it's really all about. Providing you're there and I can get up in the morning – put one foot in front of the other – I'm prepared to do it come rain, hail or shine, because some mornings it's horrible, but the majority are fantastic and there's nothing beats the birds singing and you're delivering milk and there's nobody else to bother you in the road, there's no traffic, there's no people about, that world is your own at that time in the morning.

People say I'm daft to get up in the morning at that time but I see all sorts, you'd be surprised – men coming from people's houses that they shouldn't be coming from and their secret's safe with me. We've had ladies out in the middle of the night that have actually got fed up of their husbands and they've decided to just walk out at four in the morning. It might be dark and they've seen me and think 'don't tell anybody.' I've seen one or two men coming home in their boxer shorts at night, come behind, and then I give them a fright when I go around with the milk.

People who actually enjoy your company, you become like a befriender to them. One April morning a lady says "Oh" she said, "I got a big cobweb up my stairs Pauline, d'ya think you could get it down?" So I says, "Course I can, no problem at all."

"Well, I'm afraid the brush is in that shed down the garden."

"Right" says I, "Ok, no problem, I'll go and get it then."

So off I goes for the brush, the stepladders, gets up the steps with the brush, its quite high up to the top of this thing. So anyhow, I says, "Where is this cobweb?"

"April Fool!"

"You are joking!" I said. I nearly hit her with the brush.

One lady left me a note one Saturday morning, I collect money on a Friday and a Saturday morning, and it said 'Dear Pauline, money on the table, husband in bed. Help yourself.' That wasn't too bad now. I think she meant to help myself to the money, not the husband.

Pauline Jackson, milk lady

Going to market

It used to be a nightmare of a job to take sheep because it was a small market at the back of Buxton town centre. They were metal pens and they had twenty sheep in them. You had to be there very early to get the pens. The idea was to get two sheep in each pen. If you got there early and you put ten or a dozen in the back of your vehicle and you wanted three pens, you'd put two or three in each pen until you'd finished collecting the correct number of sheep in.

We used to have an old army TK Bedford which was altered to carry sheep, with an open top and a side door on it that dropped into a shippen door, to load the sheep. We went through from about 1958 to 1964/65 taking a lot of sheep into Buxton. One particular day, we took seven loads in and six loads out. We started at a place called Frank Belfield's at three o'clock in the morning and that particular wagon held forty lambs or thirty-two ewes and we finished just after midnight delivering the last to Pieclough Farm at Longnor, behind The Winking Man. What a hell of a job we had because these army wagons have only got a quarter lock on. When we got there, there was a small stream before we went into the yard and we had tremendous difficulty in turning this lorry around at that time of night. The full proceeds for the day's work from three o'clock until after midnight was eighteen pounds. Each sheep was charged a shilling to take them from each farm into Buxton. So by the time you'd paid all your petrol out and your time out, there wasn't a lot left at the end of the day.

You know if you're among sheep all your life, it's quite easy to spot what the butcher wants or what your fellow farmer wants. They're looking for a certain quality of sheep and they're prepared to pay a good price for it. The prices then were on average about three pounds to three pounds fifty for a lamb and four pounds fifty to six pounds for a good breeding shearing ewe.

Today it's far more complicated. It's all paperwork, rules and regulations. In fact it'll take me pretty well an hour every morning. I try and keep it up to date every day, unless we're very busy, and when I come in for breakfast, the next hour is done on keeping records and filling forms in. There were no complications before. You just did your farming and that was it – you sold your animals. You'd got time to visit your next-door neighbour and have a fair bit of social life.

John Eardley, farmer

Deadweight

There was hardly any direct selling in those days, everything was sold through a market. I think the local butcher, yes, even in the 1970s, we did sell the odd animal, no sheep then, but odd cattle to the local butcher in Chapel, but on the whole, there was an awful lot more market trading than there is now; there wasn't the deadweight trading where animals are sold to go straight to the butcher off the farm. They don't go to market. The butcher or some of these bigger companies have fieldsmen who come out to see you and judge the animals. Instead of being sold on the look of the animal, as a traditional market is done, they're sold on price over the hook when they're dead, so you get so much per kilo deadweight.

Sue Jackson, farmer

Under The Hammer

I was a livestock auctioneer and I spent most of my career in Bakewell. The new Bakewell Mart was a goal we achieved after about twenty years. Bagshaws ran the Peak. I think there were seven marts, from Lichfield in the south.... Uttoxeter, Derby, Ashbourne, Bakewell, Hope and Penistone. Each had their set days of the week. Bakewell market a Monday, special sales Thursday, and fat on a Tuesday. Uttoxeter was Wednesday, Ashbourne Thursday, Hope in the season from about the end of July until Christmas would sell off fat sheep on a Wednesday, with store cattle and store sheep alternating on a Friday. Friday was Derby and Saturday was Uttoxeter, when we sold a lot of store cattle, and a lot of the farm dispersal sales would be on a Saturday. The special sheep sales were in the Autumn. It's still like that, except that quite a few centres, like Ashbourne, Uttoxeter and Macclesfield have closed: economics – it's now in fewer hands, like every other business.

When I first started we stuck a number on it and sold it. Now there's endless forms and identification of individual animals, all that sort of thing, which has

40 The livestock ring at Bakewell Market, 2005 © Sheila Hine

made it a lot more difficult. If a farmer got up that morning and decided to sell a cow, he could. Now if he's brought something onto the holding within the last six days he can't sell it through a livestock market. It has to go direct to the abattoir, it can't go to another farm. That's a disease regulation, which came from Foot and Mouth.

When I first came to Bakewell Mart in 1963, a thousand sheep would be a big day. They have anything up to five thousand now, partly because they have the accommodation to house them now. They couldn't house them in those days and the market was in the centre of the town etc. But we would sell seven or eight hundred sheep. We would have up to twenty or thirty retailers from Chesterfield and Sheffield, well, wholesale butchers from Sheffield and retailers from Buxton and Matlock. We ran sheep sales, collective store sheep sales from all over the Peak Park, at Hartington. Our biggest sale at Hartington was just over twenty-five thousand sheep. I sold all the sheep at the Chatsworth Sheep Sale for thirty-five years, which, when it started was the biggest sale in the UK for a single owner.

Ian Lawton, auctioneer

Village Shop

The shop sold virtually everything you could think of. It would have been our front room. We had groceries, sweets, chocolate, paraffin, bread – which was kept in a cupboard next to the paraffin – yeast, anything that anyone would want. It was all packed into this tiny place, and we were quite busy, I guess. I used to love helping out and I suppose I was in and out from being tiny, because what else could they do with me? They had to keep an eye on me so I used to help from the time I learnt to count. My favourite sweets were fish mixtures, little boiled sweets with pink fishes, I liked those, they were a sort of pear-drop really. There were sweets in jars, chocolates, things like that.

41 A 1950s village shop, recreated at Ryedale Folk Museum, 2007
© Lynne Mycock

The shop was chaos, because there was a lot packed in. There was a big counter which divided the shop. There were the customers on one side and us on the other and you served everybody, there was no self-service or anything like that. We had scales on the counter and a sort of step-like system built on the end that my dad used to put jars of sweets on. The counter itself was plain on the customer's side, with drawers on the front and a cupboard underneath. The second drawer down was always the money drawer because we had no till or anything like that, and it had to be out of the reach of customers. The other drawers had various things in them; one had boot laces – all the paperwork got pushed into the top drawer – and tobacco was in the bottom drawer. There were things everywhere, it was quite small, only about twelve feet square. There were shelves all along one side, which I used to stack tins on. I used to like making patterns with the tins, but they never stayed like that for long because they'd always get untidy.

Joan Stewartson, housewife

Post Office Closure

Mum had the local shop and post-office. She was always in the house even when the shop was open, for the simple reason the shop and the house were all part of the same building. In fact to go upstairs from the living room you used to have to walk through the shop. It was rather an odd set-up compared with today, because every customer had to wait for my mum or my brother or me to fetch the items they wanted to the counter. They couldn't actually get immediate access to the items by just walking round grabbing them – not at all like shopping nowadays. There'd be rush-hour times. People would bring their kids along to get on the school bus and pop in the shop. I don't remember the shop being shut at lunchtimes at all; mum was in the house anyway, she'd just hear the bell and serve whoever turned up. There weren't too many people who were calling who were strangers unless it was a weekend, so they'd just turn up and be on Christian name terms. Later on in an afternoon'd be busy till it closed five o'clock, half-past five. When we left Hassop in 1970, the shop closed and it was also the post-office. It closed permanently when we left the village. It wasn't taken on by anybody else so that was the end of an era, really. It was sold off as a private dwelling, built in 1675, and been developed very nicely since. It's now called Postman's Knock, appropriate given that the letterbox is still in the wall of the house.

42 Wall Postbox, Hassop, 2008
© Damian Hughes

Michael Pearson, farmer's son

Packaging

Butter came in big forty pound blocks and a chap cut a piece off, put it on a piece of greaseproof paper, weighed it, made it up with a bit more or took a bit off to the right weight, wrapped it up and that was it. None of this packaging we have today. Same with bacon – you put a piece on the slicer, wound the handle and you got two or three slices, whatever you wanted and you weighed it and that was it. Sugar? Came in big bags, you weighed it out into small blue bags. Everything was done locally, not like it is today where everything is pre-packed in a central place. Half the problem we've got now with landfill sites is because of the packaging. Why does stuff need to be not only packed just once but twice and sometimes three times? It's absolutely ridiculous.

Ray Platts, farmer

43 Today's supermarket packaging, 2008 © Damian Hughes

Skidmores' Greengrocers, Bakewell

With their brother John, Michael and Graham Skidmore were the greengrocers on Matlock Street, Bakewell until they retired in 2006. It was the quintessential old-fashioned market town shop, rightly renowned in Bakewell and beyond. Michael's account is in roman typescript; Graham's in italics.

Me dad came out of the army I think about 1918 after being invalided out. He got shot in the First World War. Me mother used to help him run the shop but me dad died in 1946. When I left school, I started working in the shop straightaway when I were fourteen. I didn't want to but I had to really. I took it in me stride. *I start-ed when I were twelve helping me dad in the shop. Filling up, putting all the bananas out. All the bananas were in straw in them days in little boxes, like a coffin. And there was all funny little creatures and these beetles and everything, and spiders. Me mother once got a snake out of a banana box. She put it on' back of fire to get rid of it. She were terrified!*

We used to get fish direct from mostly Grimsby, and Hull. Sometimes they'd bring it in the night, drop it off in the shop doorway about one or two o'clock in the morning. It used to be there for next morning when we wanted it. We used to get big blocks of ice on the fish wagon from Grimsby. We had a big sink in the shop, we had a block of ice in the shop and we used to use that to put the fish on and whatnot. Then we got a fridge later on and, you know, it's all changed a bit.

We used to keep a lot of birds ourselves...hens, geese, turkeys. *Goose eggs. We sold one hundred in one day. We used to have a marvellous trade for goose eggs.*

44 Skidmores of Bakewell, Graham and Michael Skidmore outside their shop, 1990s
© Courtesy Michael Skidmore

And duck eggs. We used to sell guinea fowl eggs, quail eggs. People thought they were a delicacy but they weren't as nice as a guinea fowl egg actually. They used to make Fabergé goose eggs. Some people used to come and buy twenty or thirty at a time. They'd make these trinket boxes. *And somebody brought us an ostrich egg in' shop.* We've sold one or two ostrich eggs. Sold them about six pounds each. *Haddon Hall were making a film, Jane Eyre, and they came and bought everything off us.* They bought goose eggs to put on show in the old-fashioned kitchen when they were doing *Pride and Prejudice* or something at the time.

Somebody once brought a tawny owl into' shop and I had it fifteen years before it died.

It had been knocked down by a car and he said "Oh, I think it'll die" but I managed to bring it round and I used to feed it with bits of pheasant and all sorts, you know, pheasant giblets and I'd got plenty of offal from the shop to feed it on and it lived fifteen years, that's very unusual for a tawny owl to live that long. We do still keep some birds actually, not a lot though now. It's just a hobby, the hens and geese. John, me brother, he were marvellous at plucking chickens. He used to do that up at the field and bring them down. He worked in the background, he didn't like serving in the shop. We had this place in the back-yard where we used to hang the poultry. You just had to see what you could sell and just kill enough to tide you over that time when you could sell them.

People went for oranges a big lot in winter, with colds and flu and what not. Oranges were a big sale, big Jaffas in those days as well, not like nowadays. Same as asparagus. Certain people only bought that, and some people never even heard of it, never even tried asparagus. It was always potatoes, carrots, onions, swedes, parsnips, celery in winter. But in the summer when June came, we used to get a lot of local strawberries off different people. They used to go very well. And blackcurrants, redcurrants. *And gooseberries, gooseberries went ever so well. I went picking bilberries on Stanton Moor. I got loads.* Bananas are easy to eat I think. People just thought, "Well, I'll take a banana, pack me husband off to work, I'll put a couple of bananas in and that'll keep him quiet." *And mushrooms, we used to go and get field mushrooms. We used to get millions.* Blue Stalk Morels. We knew where all them come round Bakewell... I knew what they were like, you can smell Blue Stalks before you get to them. In a field, they either grow in a straight line or a circle. It's marvellous finding them, it's ever so interesting. Some Sunday mornings we used to go out and we used to get about a stone weight and they used to sell like hotcakes. Anybody with a garden would bring stuff in. They'd come in the shop and say "I've got a dozen spare lettuce, would you like them?" so we used to have them, whatever they'd got to spare. You were only talking about shillings then.

We used to sell cows in the Bakewell Market about forty years ago. We used to keep about forty at one time. We didn't count ourselves as farmers but we kept quite a few cows. We'd drive them down the road to Bakewell Market. We slowly got rid of all the cows. Too much trouble, you get older, you can't do with all the hassle and that can you? And all the paperwork involved with the cattle nowadays, it's unbelievable. *We've got a big cow on the field, a marvellous cow, about eleven year old. The biggest one in England! We just go and feed her every morning and look after her well. Everybody says she's the biggest one in England* .

We had an old-fashioned bike with a carrier and I used to take the orders out. I used to go all over Bakewell, everywhere, taking orders. I knew every place in Bakewell more or less in those days. Me dad had a van, he used to go round the villages at one time and then he packed that in and he just concentrated on the shop, you know, but people come from round all the villages in Bakewell. Same as now, I can't go out without people don't stop me and say, "How are you getting on?" We had some very nice customers. Three-quarters would be women who shopped in the shop but certain men did the shopping for their wives and you got to know them as well. Certain men get stuck in their ways and they've got to do it, they didn't like trusting their wives to do it! Lady Elizabeth, the Duke of Devonshire's sister, brought John Betjeman and introduced me to him one day. She brought no end of people in. *We've had Cliff Richards (sic) looking in' window. He was going to Chatsworth. He said, "What a marvellous shop yours is." We supplied all the hotels in Bakewell. The Rutland used to trade off us. Every hotel in Bakewell came in our shop.* Everybody was very sociable.

The game really made the shop very famous. Pheasants were better 'cause they hung for about a fortnight at least. Rabbits, you used to hang those up as well and get rid of them. When the weather was warm you'd got to get rid of them quick. You'd got to know what you were doing. A lot of farmers used to get these pheasants come on their land from different estates and they used to say "Well, it's a shame to shoot them just for meself, I've got what I want, I'll just take one or two down to Michael at the shop." We used to sell a lot of rabbits. We used to get a lot of rabbits local. We used to know all the farmers roundabout and they used to be only too pleased to go and shoot a few rabbits and bring them in the shop. It made them a few shilling and made me a few shilling as well. I had no trouble selling those... and hares. I used to hang rabbits outside the shop or the game and people used to say "I'll have that rabbit third from the end". They liked coming picking those, which I didn't mind – you'd got to sell them. Same as pheasants, you'd get some people go 'round twenty brace of pheasants and pick the biggest brace. When we got the stuff hanging outside the shop, all day long people were taking photographs. Everybody seen the photographs. Everybody. Pictures have been in all the papers in England, everywhere...National Geographic, all sorts of magazines and people come in from America and say "I've seen a picture of your shop in a doctor's surgery somewhere". We've had people from Canada, Australia. *They used to come from all over' world taking photographs of' shop. We were famous. They played a band outside the shop on carnival day and they got me and Michael to stand outside the shop and they took photographs, everybody were taking photographs. They called us 'Heroes of Bakewell'.*

They stopped us hanging all the birds up later on in years. Couldn't hang anything outside. You had to be ever so careful in the shop, how you hung stuff, you couldn't have anything hanging down over anything else. It really got too much in the end I think. *They were always coming round and checking up what you're doing, keeping a watch over you all the time.* In a way, we were glad to finish... in the end, yeh. *Yeh.*

I was seventy-five when I packed in. I've been in' shop all me life so I think that was enough. We got this nice flat offered us here so we thought we'd come out of it. *We thought we'd retire. People say "Oh we do miss you now you've retired". They still stop us.* Every time you go out, people still say that to me, "Miss your shop". Well they do, it was an old-fashioned shop you see, old-fashioned people in it as well...

Graham and Michael Skidmore, greengrocers

45 Fresh fruit on display in a Bakewell greengrocer's shop today, 2008 © Damian Hughes

Shopping

Another total difference is a lot of grocers, for instance, would deliver. They had their vehicles to do that with when a lot of houses wouldn't have had cars and couldn't travel, apart from bus. Now everybody has probably got access to a vehicle and everyone drives as soon as they are able to. The difficulty within towns is, of course, supermarkets have got there and it's difficult for others to

46 Taylor's Fruiterer's Van delivering at Calver, c.1930
© Courtesy of Mrs J Gregory and www.picturethepast.org.uk

survive. That's a sad thing, I think. There could be more consideration given to how the planners look at supermarkets and large hypermarkets in rural towns, because all the rest of them are small shops and cannot survive, so the variety and the livings of people in market town centres becomes totally changed, probably for the worse.

Tony Kemish, farmer

Bakewell Co-Op

I would say that about 10% of our produce is from the local area although we try and keep a lot, probably 40 to 50%, depending on season, British. Our movement, the Midlands Co-op is trying to make sure that the majority of our produce, beef, pork, chicken are all from British farms where we do have some of our own farms in the country.

What about recycling?
In the last two years it's got a bigger concern. We offer a biodegradable bag and our cardboard and our plastic all gets recycled. I suppose more emphasis on your home recycling needs to be better, as well as combining it with supermarkets.

Do you have much of a direct input into local farming?
As a store – no, that's all done from our head office. We're given a listing of range

47 Manager Neil Styring
with customer
"supporting Shop mobility"
© Courtesy Midlands
Co-operative Society

47 The Co-op Supermarket, Bakewell, 2008 © Damian Hughes

and we draw from the depot. I wouldn't say we compete with farmers markets because we offer a daily, weekly, yearly product all the time, whereas the Bakewell Farmers' Market is the last Saturday of every month. I'd like to think that we are part of the community. We're very community based as far as staffing and the local area. I'm a member of the local Chamber of Trade for Bakewell, so you do get to see other perspectives of business, not just our own.

It's probably slightly different here because you get a lot of tourists coming to Bakewell. So no, I suppose it is somewhat unique here – you can get any style of customer coming in from any area, whether it be Britain, Europe, Brazil – they have heard of Bakewell and they come and visit. Local products are more for specialist shops you've got around the town – like Bakewell pudding parlours that target tourists because it's part of Bakewell's history. With the town itself being a bit more traditional I'd like to think most local people cook from scratch, but there is an element of convenience.

Cookery programmes skew purchasing. If Jamie Oliver has done... can't really think of one off the top of my head, but maybe he's done something on chicory – then all of a sudden, chicory, we've sold out within a day whereas probably one case would last a whole week. Where I worked in Leicestershire before, there was a local honey manufacturer where we used to buy a large quantity of honey. That's just one example that I've come into contact with. We've certainly not done anything in Bakewell yet. I think we've been asked for oatcakes in the past, which Somerfield used to stock. I can pass that on to our marketing people at head office but it's not been taken forward as such yet. It's a question of volume. You've got to have the supplier that can stock not just one store of the Midland Society but all of our two hundred stores. But our head office marketing department's always looking for new avenues to go down and new ranges to have a look at.

Neil Styring, store manager

Chatsworth Farm Shop

A view from the late eighties

In the early 1970s the in-hand farm at Chatsworth was doing very badly. Everything seemed to conspire against it and the accounts made depressing reading. Each section was losing money and the Jersey herd at the Stud Farm was becoming an expensive luxury. At about that time I became associated with the Royal Smithfield Show, run by that happy triumvirate of farmers, butchers and agricultural-machinery makers. Listening to the farmers and butchers talking made me want to sell our produce direct to the consumer so as to help the farm through extra returns made by cutting out the middle man. The home freezer boom was at its height and every householder seemed bent on owning one, so why not sell our beef and lamb directly off the land where they were bred, add

48 Chatsworth Farm Shop, 2007 © Chatsworth Estate

dairy produce from the Jersey herd, venison from the park deer, pheasants, vegetables – the possibilities seemed endless. A farm shop might be the answer, an offshoot of the farm itself.

The idea got a lukewarm reception in the Estate Office. A farm shop was a new venture. The patient Derrick Penrose and company were slowly converted, and I hasten to say have given their whole-hearted support ever since... Eventually in 1976 planning permission was granted... All went well for a time and the customers were pleased with their meat. The first major difficulty was continuity of supply. There are enough lambs to feed an army from June to October, and then there are none. Naturally the customers did not appreciate this, so they went to Sainsbury's where lamb is for ever and knows no seasons.

It was not a happy situation, and our turnover suffered accordingly. The shop began to lose money and by the beginning of 1984 there had been four years of escalating losses. The trustees got restive. They said if it does not turn round in two years it must stop trading. It was very depressing after so much effort had gone into it.

We made radical changes. Management was switched from the Farms to Victoria Edward's Retail Sales Department. We asked for planning permission to sell bought-in meat and other foods, preferably local and always British. After what seemed an endless wait, it was granted. Perhaps one of the reasons was that in a time of high un-employment seven jobs would have been lost had the shop closed.... We were lucky in that our chef, Jean-Pierre Béraud, passionately wanted to run a shop. He had no retailing experience but has a blinkered interest in food and quality, plus a Frenchman's instinct for business. He was appointed manager in 1984 and there was an immediate change in fortunes. From a loss of £31,000 in 1983 Jean-Pierre pulled it round into profit in the following twelve months.

Having made jam, marmalade, scones and cakes in our own kitchen for the shop, and having kept meticulous accounts with every ounce of flour costed, Jean-Pierre understood the demand for cooked food, so he made a kitchen next to the shop where patés, hams, cakes, biscuits and several kinds of bread were made, wafting irresistible smells throughout the building.

The Duchess of Devonshire
The Estate: *A View from Chatsworth*, Macmillan 1990 p219-221

Farmers' Markets

I'm probably keeping less adult animals but I'm keeping all the progeny through to finish, because, with doing the farmer's markets, I want to retail the beef. Obviously the return, although you've got the animal for two-and-a-half years, rather than six months, the retail margin is greater than you would get from selling a suck calf.

I now keep Dexter cattle, which are smaller. I can keep more of them on the same acreage, because they don't chew the ground as much since they're not as big and heavy. Dexters are a native breed and very herdy animals; they do like living in family groups. And as far as the retail side of it's concerned it's easier because they yield a smaller joint which is what people on market stalls tend to like better than the big joints they get off the big commercials. So it was partly a commercial decision, partly environmental, to keep the smaller cattle.

Farmers are becoming much better, much more market orientated. I think we always used to depend on the local livestock market, and if we didn't like the price we brought them home and tried again next week or what-have-you. But I think we are getting more in touch with the final customer. Take farmers' markets: twenty years ago if I said to a local farmer I was going to a farmers' market and selling my own produce they'd have thought I'd gone crackers, whereas now they'd say, 'Oh, are you?' So everybody, even the old traditional farmers are coming round to the fact that you really can do this. I'm thinking, yeah, because my whole end result goes onto the stall at the farmer's market, the whole farming is worked backwards from that. I need a certain amount of pigs on a certain day, or a pig a week or what-ever, so it works backwards, whereas before I think we were working the other way

49 Bakewell Farmers' Market, 2008 © Lynne Mycock and Damian Hughes

round: Oh gosh, my pig's had a litter of pigs, I'm going to have to sell them. It's working the other way round, it's much more market orientated.

I'm in a mini-cooperative, in a farmers' market, I'm cooperating, collaborating with a colleague, with another farmer and we're doing farmers' markets together. It's working very well at the moment. I've got more acreage and they've got more food skills, so we put the two together. They make delicatessen type things, like salami and pancetta and all these things which add value to my produce. Back in the 1970s nobody would buy a chorizo sausage, they wouldn't dare. I mean, pork and leek was pretty dangerous! They make salami, they do air dried hams, they make sausages, all sorts of continental sausages. Well I couldn't do that, because I haven't got the skill.

Sue Jackson, farmer

Peak Choice

A new scheme's just started which covers the whole of the Peak District called Peak Choice. It was launched a few weeks ago by Prince Charles and again we've got a couple of tenants involved with about ten farmers working together at this stage – internet sales, marketing their meat, marketing their beef or lamb or pork over the internet backed by Prince Charles. The benefit is you're pulling together to set that steady supply up – people don't realise if you want a joint of beef it's a three year process. You've got to breed the animal, two and a half years fattening, butchering, hang it for three or four weeks to get the best quality – so when people come to me and say we are interested in you supplying us with beef in our restaurant, you know it takes time to set up as well as market that steady supply.

Russell Ashfield, National Trust

Poaching in the early Sixties

The devil makes work for idle hands

I was in a building partnership with my friend. We had a joiners shop at Over Haddon and were working for ourselves, you see, and found ourselves with quite a bit of spare time. We didn't do enough work, too busy poaching.

We used to make things. We made a device for pulling pheasants out of the trees. It was a pole about twelve to fifteen foot long. We ran a wire up the pole and stapled it in position so that it was movable. We formed a loop and that loop slid over the head of the pheasant and down its neck. We used to put it over the pheasants as they perched in the trees and then pull them out. They usually stayed quite still while roosting. This was in Lathkill Dale. It'd be too easy to spot us in the daytime, so we'd go after dark with our pole. It was a long job so we used to go in the dead of night. Eventually we were frightened away because the gamekeeper realised there was something going off. What he'd done was tie a plastic fertiliser bag in the trees at about every ten yards. When the breeze came these shapes were moving in the trees and it really scared us off. So we had to abandon that.

We always used to be getting hares and rabbits. We'd shoot the rabbits. And once we got a stag. I always used to carry the gun in the cab when we were doing the poaching. I was going home one night through Hassop and we got going over the hills to the other side towards Calver and there was a steep bank with trees and everything. I was driving nice and steady like, as I was always looking for things in the wood, mainly pheasants. This stag galloped down the wood and jumped straight into the middle of the road in front of me, which was an ideal opportunity. So that had to be shot.

My friend lived in Cressbrook Mill and down by the side of the mill were all the fish ponds where Chatsworth use to rear fish before they put them in the river. We used to watch them growing and used to feed them, you see. Then we went one night and we emptied it. We got the lot. We had well over a hundred-weight of fish. It was strange, nobody saw us. We were over the fence and in by the pond where they were feeding and we were fishing them out about four o'clock in the morning. They were so easy to catch because they were feeding them on pellets you see, fish pellets. So as soon as we threw the line in with the bread on and as soon as they heard the splash, they didn't care what it was, they came and took it and we were pulling in six, seven, eight at a time. Marvellous big fish. Two, three, four or five pounders. A police car pulled up at the side of the fence, looked through and didn't spot us. They had a look and just drove on and we were stacking fish up one after another. It was an exciting one with the fish. That was great. All night. We got so many in. But nobody saw us. We didn't go back again. We did it once.

We had a little builder's truck too. We used to ride around Chatsworth and when we were driving we would pick out the pheasants in the wood and shoot them. We always stayed in the vehicle, you see. We shot from the cab. We'd slow down when we got to the pheasant and one of us would shoot it and just leave it. We never picked them up; we just left them there in case we were stopped. We used to go round and pick them up later. That was the idea: not to get caught for poaching. I knew a lot of poachers who were doing it but we never actually encountered them when we were out.

We had a little diagram. We knew all the roads and we just marked where we shot one then we went back and collected it. We just gave them to friends. We weren't out to make any money out of it. We just enjoyed the poaching, that was the thing: – the thrill of it. We did that for quite a while. It seemed to be good at the time until I was marched off down the road by a six foot six bobby and my feet weren't touching the ground.

Well, obviously the spotted us to tip the police off, but we didn't think we'd been seen. We found ourselves on Hassop roundabout near the thirteen bends. We were surrounded by six police cars and we were arrested.

We didn't have any pheasants at all, you see, we never picked them up. We had a couple of guns in the cab and they took us to Bakewell police station and locked us up. They put us in different rooms and interviewed us separately and asked the old question: what were we doing and where'd we got these guns and everything. And in fact, while I was there, the phone kept ringing and it was Chatsworth calling up to try and make sure they arrested us and summoned us. They brought the guns in, checked them all over and everything, and just carried on with the interview. We denied everything. We'd say, 'Where's the evidence? We haven't touched any pheasants.' We never got done for the poaching.

We got a summons for having the gun but they never could do us for poaching because we didn't have anything with us. I got fined ten shillings and I think my friend got done for about two pounds. It was nothing really. After we got caught, we daren't go out with a gun again. It would have been a serious offence.

Anonymous, poacher

The Gamekeeper

Poaching

People don't really poach any more, but having said that, when I was up in Wigan we had Liverpool on one side of us and Wigan on the other and a lot of scallies. In some areas you still get trouble and it's got nastier over the years. I mean before, it used to be one for the pot but now it's organised gangs and things can get very violent and very nasty. You've got to be prepared for that.

I really only have trouble with fish poachers in the summer but they're not trying to net the river or anything like that. They're only going to catch a few fish so generally it's a case of moving them on and warning them with the police, but we don't very often have to prosecute. Deer poaching is still a big thing, as deer fetch quite a lot of money. A big red deer carcass can get you a few hundred pounds so that's the only one where poachers are alive and kicking in a big way. I suppose salmon poaching as well, but deer is the biggie. Hare-coursing was nasty and still is when it takes place. But of course, since the hunting ban hare-coursing has gone right down. Legally they are no longer allowed to hunt with dogs. I know it still goes on, but not to the extent it used to. Since the ban I haven't heard or seen anyone.

Pheasant Rearing

I rear and release pheasants. I've got six thousand birds. We've got fifteen hundred acres; about six hundred acres woodland and the rest surrounding grassland. Most of the shooting is concentrated in the woodland, but we utilise all the grassland. I

50 Alec Neville, Gamekeeper, 2008 © Lynne Mycock

get them as poults at the end of June, between six and eight weeks old. I rear them in very big large pens, check for diseases, feed them on pellets at first and move them onto wheat gradually. After two or three weeks I start to let them out of the pen. Once out they are more or less completely free range and they can do what they want. We have to do 'dogging in' which is basically when the birds start wandering towards the boundaries, we drive them back. We do that probably two or three times a day, depending on what time of year. It's also a matter of feeding the birds every single day. As the weather gets colder they come back into the woods. We'll bring the feeders into the woods and the pheasants come back with them – hopefully.

Vermin

There's a lot of vermin control: foxes, crows, magpies.... foxes are the big one. I've had about fifty killed one night but I've been on other estates where we've lost two or three hundred in a night just from a single fox. When we get the poults they're really vulnerable and we'll be out with the high-powered lamp and rifle two or three times a week – lamping foxes. We don't do snaring here. I have a red filter so it doesn't scare the foxes much. You just shine it over the field and fox's eyes reflect back at you. You get to learn what a fox's eyes look like as opposed to a sheep's. When you see it, you've got to try and get within range or bring the fox to you, which you can do by trying to imitate a hare or a rabbit in distress to bring it in that way. Some people have tape recordings of other foxes barking, being as foxes are territorial, they sometimes come to them. We probably go out and see ten foxes and shoot two. Sometimes we have trouble with owls – they'll take a few out of the release pen, but it's only for a week while they're quite small. Sparrow-hawks, goshawks – they'll all take a few but we turn six thousand pheasants out, they're not going to make much of a dent on that. Live and let live. It's really not a problem to me.

The Shoot

The pheasant shooting season starts on the first of October and runs through to the first of February. We shoot any day apart from Sundays and Christmas Day. We shoot once a week. We kill between one hundred and two hundred and fifty birds in a day. Nine guns shooting. From last year, new regulations were brought in. We all had to go on a game-handling course so now we are actually professional hunters and we have a little card. All the birds now are handled properly, we chill down to four degrees, they're hung in there overnight, and the day after they're with the game dealer. The guns normally take a brace, the beaters – their job is to drive the pheasants – normally take a brace and then what's left goes to the dealers.

Economics

A pheasant poult at six weeks old costs me three pounds each. To get to shooting age is approximately another pound a bird. Six thousand birds... so about twenty four thousand pounds outlay. When we shoot the pheasants at the start of the season, you'll probably be getting about two pounds a brace – two birds. By the end of the season you'll be down possibly to thirty pence a brace. Although we are having a very good season this year my profit from the sale of game will probably touch a thousand pounds. So for a twenty-four grand outlay I get a thousand pound back which isn't brilliant but, obviously, we are not farming the animal for the meat, and game prices are terrible. Game shooting is huge at the moment. There are shoots springing up all over. We have a syndicate with nine guns, I could fill those twice over tomorrow if need be.

Shaped to Shoot

There's public everywhere in the countryside so we have to talk to them, liaise with them. You get a few that want to shout abuse and have a go at you. What they don't realise is that we've shot here for over a hundred years and this dale, the woodland especially, has been shaped to shoot. The rivers have been looked after for fishing and the woods for shooting – it's the same all over the country. All the big estates are planted really for shooting. People think it's been planted for them to go rambling around, but it wasn't, it was planted for shooting.

Cooking

I do a lot of cooking at home. I like trying different things to do with pheasants. The thing with pheasants is people don't eat it because they think it's some exotic beast. If you talk to anyone about pheasants they say, "Oh it tastes really strong doesn't it?" And they don't know what to do with it. People cook it too much. They dry it out – you only want to roast it for about twenty minutes. Game is pink as well and people don't like the idea of serving bird-meat 'pink,' but it's absolutely fine with pheasant. It's a lot better, but people overcook it and it gets dry and tough. Pheasant cooked badly is bloody awful but pheasant cooked well is just fantastic!

Alec Neville, gamekeeper

Mick Shirt, Master Butcher Critchlow's Farm Shop, Bakewell

I started my farming/butchering career when I was about twelve. When I left school it was a natural progression to go into a butcher's shop. My first job was at Norman Gibbs in Tideswell. I'm a Tideswell lad really. People don't believe I was very shy, but I was really shy and I remember on a couple of occasions they asked me to go in the shop and I went home instead. I really did. I could be very awkward, you know!

Now I manage Critchlows in Bakewell. The Critchlow family have actually been butchering in Bakewell for about 120 years prior to Mr and Mrs Brocklehurst taking the shop over.

People in rural communities still want black pudding and pig's trotters and all the old-fashioned products like brawn. We still sell plenty of brawn, things like that. People haven't lost their taste for it. In fact a lot of the younger people want to try them. A lot of the modern delis are reintroducing these things and making out it's something new. Well it's nothing new. I think we're very fortunate. We've got a local customer-base, a very loyal following, so we don't have any trouble. Obviously at spring and summer we've got an extra influx of tourists so it helps us as well.

Pie making was just another feather in my cap. You've learned your sausage making and you've done your black pudding making and you think, I'll have a go at pie making. If you're interested in doing the job you want to do everything. So that's what you do – it's a passion. The first prize I won was the best black pudding in Great Britain. It was in 1987 up at Bolton which was a good prize because that's the home of the black pudding, so I was very pleased with that. Since then I've won numerous nationwide prizes for pies and sausage and haslet and in 2007, I won a gold medal at the Great Taste Awards down at London for my dry-cured bacon.

51 Mick Shirt, Critchlows, Bakewell, 2007 © Courtesy Michael Shirt

I think basic pie making – anybody can do. There are just one or two secret ingredients which I wouldn't divulge to anybody. It's very funny, I could give you my pie recipe and all the secret ingredients but you probably couldn't put it together and end up with the same product. It's like making a cake – you can give someone a recipe but it never turns out the same, does it?

Sticking to quality is imperative. I think it's going back to sourcing your own meat, off your own farm or local market so it's maintaining the high quality, and making your products out of that meat is all you can do. Quality will always win through on price.

Mick Shirt, master butcher

The Butcher's Window

The local butcher had the meat hanging in the window, so he cut off the pieces that you wanted, all the carcasses were hanging in the window, and I can remember them getting a fridge put in, which was really quite something. A big walk-in fridge.

Sue Jackson, farmer

52 Meat on the hook. Wheeldon's butchers in Buxton, 1930s © Courtesy Roy Mycock

Arnold Mycock & Sons, Butchers, Buxton

We've always done our own butchering. We've bought cattle out of Bakewell and Chelford and Leek but the majority of what my father has bought or reared has been with the intention of going through the shop.

No. 7 Market Street, Buxton was where my father kicked off, with a hundred pound which he borrowed off my mother. He never needed it 'cause everybody knew where he was going to trade 'cause he went with a man called Bill Thompson. He was the man that Dad took the business off and he said, "I'll stick with you for a fortnight, Arnold, make sure you're okay and introduce you to the customers and then you can move on."

He stayed for six years with me dad, 'cause he loved him to bits, and me Dad loved Bill, and it was only when he died that he finished. Mr Thompson, taught me how to slaughter and how to conduct meself. When you're wild as a child you know, you don't want shop-work and people are a nuisance. But he said "Look, you've got to do it, got to do it..." He persevered with me that much I thought, "Sod it, I'll do it then."

In the old days it was fantastic. We used to go to Bakewell to buy the cattle on a Monday morning. We used to take them over or they'd be delivered to Chelmorton. A little slaughterhouse owned by Dennis Needham and they'd rest there and then I used to go over there on the bike and bed them down, straw them down until next day. Then they'd be slaughtered in the evening or after the shop had shut on the Tuesday evening.

Now today, it's a different story. You've got to find a slaughterhouse that really wants you. There's not the care and attention that was paid years ago. Because years ago, you used to go around butchers shops, and have a look at how they dressed their animals and I would like to think that I dressed ours better than anybody else's, but obviously they'd come round and see if they'd dressed theirs better than ours.

The rapport in all of that was unbelievable because we all wanted to be the best. When my father first started he thought we'd never last five minutes, but we've more about us than that and I kept spurring my father on, probably in a direction he didn't want to go, but he did and we drove on and drove on and drove on until we got where we are today.

In the family we've all got our different roles. I don't know what my role is now but my daughter does all the bookwork, serves in the shop. My brother does the buying and I do the selling of the meat, working out the prices and working out what's happening and alter things if need be. But it's a lesser role than my

53 The Butcher's Window, Arnold Mycock, Buxton, 1982 © Courtesy Roy Mycock

daughter and my brother, they are the major players. I was a major player at one time but now I'm only a lesser player, but an important player as they rely on me for the final decision. That's the way we carry on, like my father did with me. Just the same.

On the farm we've got a thousand calves, sheep, lambs, we've got pigs. We've got an ample supply if things went wrong to keep the shop going for six months without going outside. I've just joined this "BioBest" scheme. I've had all my cows tested, and all my calves to make sure they are 100% healthy. I always have the vet, he comes and inspects things for me and I talk to him a lot. You couldn't manage without the vet because they are very, very good. We try and keep a closed herd so we don't buy anything at all and keep producing our own at all times.

In the old days, there were no fridges at all. We used to kill the animals and let them cool off correctly and then bring them to the shop the day after and hang them up. There used to be a firm in Buxton that made ice. It gave off the coolness that kept the sides of beef and the pigs and the sheep, cool. But there's none of that today because there's no ice works. Today it's all fridges which I don't think keep things the same as they did then, because unless you've got it in a plastic bag today, or a fridge, it doesn't keep at all.

We've got a lovely shop. Fantastic custom, fantastic people. Going back to the early days when Foot and Mouth broke out and when they had BSE, people stuck by us through thick and thin. So I thought the only thing I could do was to stick by them as well. So we've just stuck with the best and done whatever we

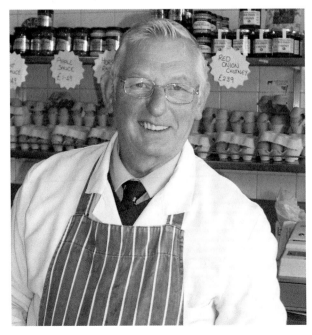

54 Roy Mycock today, Mycocks Butchers, Buxton 2008 © Andréa Lewis

possibly could do to help people in any way we could and they in turn patronised us and supported us, genuinely and openly and honestly.

When the BSE came out people were quite concerned. Red meat was a no-goer. I decided that we can't give in and what we'd do is cook some pies. So we decided to cook some meat and put 'em in some pies and sell 'em.

A lady came back and she said "Roy, I've been listening to the television." and I said, "Yes," and she says, "People are on about red meat – but I cut into my pie the other night and it was brown, so I'm clear aren't I?"

"Course you are!"

There's still a big market for black puddings. We'll sell probably fifty pound a week, tripe will do twenty pound a week, brawn probably twenty pound a week. Potted meat is a massive seller, that is sixty, eighty pound a week. Easy to spread on bread, you see.

We are never going to be as big as supermarkets. No, we've got a different clientele. The supermarkets are what they are so what you have to do is re-address all your system and go the way you know best, and hope. All we're wanting is a living, we're not wanting mega-bucks, we're just wanting a living and that's all.

I've had the best life, I've had the best mother and father I could ever have. I've had kicks up when I've needed it and I've had handshakes when I've needed it. And when we've done bad, my dad has never ever been anything but there, you know. I try my best. My Dad's been proper with me and I'll do my very, very best with my children.

We've got a lovely little business built up on a good name, good product and fair dealing. If you have got a passion for it, it bloody grows, you can't get rid of it!

Roy Mycock, master butcher

MacFisheries, Buxton

I started work at MacFisheries in Buxton at fourteen and as soon as you got there you had an immediate inspection on your hands and your nails. I was trained up by a chap called Mr Charles, Charles Wilcox. It was a sin to say to a lady that walked in the shop "Yes, love?" It had to be "Good morning, Madam – how can I help you?" That's how it had to be in the old days.

There were fifteen of us in the shop and it was split with massive marble slabs down the centre aisle. On the left hand side, as you went in, was the fruit and vegetable area – that was where the young ladies worked. We had three girls in the office and myself, the leading hand as he was called was second to Mr Charles. There were a couple of others and we did the fish and poultry side of it. We also used to have two lads from Buxton College, as it was then, to come in and do the cleaning down.

55 Buxton MacFisheries 1960s
© Courtesy Derbyshire County Council, Buxton Museum and Art Gallery, from the Board Collection

There was an old chap called Jim Booth and we used to go to Manchester market twice a day in a Morris Commercial. We started at three in the morning. Sam Hooper, who had a fish shop on Hardwick Street, couldn't drive so he had to have his fish delivered by train. He'd send somebody up there and they'd come down with this blooming great big railway truck down Station Approach. Nine times out of ten, due to the weight of the fish on board, they were eight-stone boxes, it used to run away with the person and tip up. You'd get fish spread half way down Station Approach. Everybody used to dive in and help themselves and run off with the fish.

I could tell you a tale about a certain lady that used to come into MacFisheries. She used to have a brace of grouse, and she used to prefer them 'walking' and if they were not, they were sent back and Charles got a strong rebuke from this lady, simply because there weren't enough maggots in them! And she used to have hares. We used to do jugged hare in red wine and the hare had to be hung for about three weeks down the cellars, and again the same thing applied.

The slabs in MacFisheries, for the fish and game and stuff like that, measured thirty feet long, that's how big a shop it was. We used to get fern for the herring and the mackerel and we used to plait them all the way up the slab and then we got some choice salmon and crossed those all the way up. Then we put what we call ribbons of parsley down and we'd made bouquets out of the ferns, standing them so far up. Presentation was important.

Even in the old days, a lot of fishmongers used to use 'kidology'. I think they call it cochineal, to paint their eyes to make them red – to make them look freshly caught. The worst thing about fishmongering today is there's no selection. Some of the breeds of fish that you could buy in the late fifties, early sixties, the prime fish that you wanted, like halibut, cost a pittance; now you more or less have to take out a bank loan. When you go into the supermarket or any other fish shop out of town, they've got that glazed look. It comes in to the supermarkets in sealed boxes, deeply frozen and you leave the fish out, drop it into cold water to defrost it and it'll do that within twenty-four hours, but it'll not look the same, its not inviting.

You could give me a piece of cooked fish and I'd not need to look at it because I'd know it was fresh by the smell. There's one tip I can give you for cooking fish and that is don't kill the flavour. You can buy all the sauces and the spices but there's nothing like eating a beautiful cooked trout brushed with olive oil and then lightly dusted with plain flour, and just lightly cooked. It takes six minutes, that's all.

Albert Hall, fishmonger

Killer's Currant Bread

There was best currant bread or ordinary currant bread. There must have been more currants in the best one. When we had the chapel outings it was always Killer's. Where the old bakehouse is in Wirksworth, Killers used to have that. When there were funerals and they did the funeral teas at home, they always used to have Killers' best currant bread. It was very plain. They used to have slab cake – fruit cake done in a big slab and cut into pieces. My nephew runs it now, with the old-fashioned coke ovens. That's why it's nice, it's more like home-made.

Dorothy Prince, housewife

Learning The Trade

What made you want to go into catering?

I'm not really sure. I enjoyed it when I was a kid and I thought I could do it as a job. I've learnt how to cut veg, do a meat prep, fish, all the basic foods.

What do you think about convenience food?

I don't like it. It's horrible. I try not to have it myself but I eat good food as well. At college we don't use ready-made sauces. We make it from scratch. We do it ourselves.

Where do you see yourself in ten years time?

In a west end hotel in London. I'd like to move to Australia and do some cooking there....and just move around.

Stuart Crosbie, catering student

English Pub Grub

My speciality would be English Pub Grub, cooked to a very high standard. I don't care if its chips or steak pie, but if it's homemade and cooked to a high standard, that's my kind of food. Home-made and cooked to order. It's not come out of the freezer. It's cooked for you personally. Quality? You see with your eyes what you're buying and where you buy your food is all important. Local produce is the key to local pubs. They want local food.

Steve Brook, pub chef

The Nag's Head

It was bankrupt, it was derelict but we realised it was in the right place. Probably one of the biggest steps of my life, moving out of the comfort zone that I'd been brought up with. It's a lovely place, right in the middle of Castleton. So we opened it up and I was still coming back farming in the day and going back to the Nag's at night and helping Jenny. It enabled us to enter the world of retailing and we realised that a lot of farmers are very naïve in so much as that they just relied on

56 The Nag's Head, Castleton, 2008 © Damian Hughes

people coming and buying it. We tried various things with the Nag's Head. People only go for a silver service meal if it's your wedding anniversary or it's whatever. We needed to get people in there because it was a tourist place, two million people visiting. They're not going to come for a silver service. So we closed it down, much to everyone's disgust in Castleton, and we opened a tea rooms in the day for the tourists and carvery meals, value for money, at weekends. We had three or four staff and then suddenly we were getting quite busy so we had over a dozen working.

Being farmers, we give farmers' portions and we never hid the fact we were farmers and people loved the connection between this farmer stood with his carving knife and a big lump of beef in front of him. They expected good beef and that's what they got. It was hung well, it was sourced well. On the first Sunday I think we did seventeen carvery meals. When we left we were doing somewhere between four-fifty and five-hundred. By that time we'd been there four years, we were up to twenty-four staff. Bless them, the locals made us very welcome; although it was a hotel, they came in and they drank with us which, again, enhanced the place. That's the type of industry I like to be involved in – people come to me with a smile, not a frown.

Richard Gill, farmer

Café Nathaniel

I got to know Joan Wakefield, a wardrobe mistress at the BBC. Ever such a nice lady and she said, "Where can we eat in Buxton?"

57 The Place (formerly Café Nathaniel), Buxton © Damian Hughes 2008

I said, "There aren't any restaurants."

"How disgusting!"

"I'll take you to The Palace and we'll have lunch."

She wasn't impressed at all. "What you need to do is open a restaurant!"

Sue, my wife, was with me and she answered, "That's a good idea. We'll do it!"

That's how we came into catering. Long time ago now.

I buy fruit and veg from Smithfield Market in Manchester and a bit locally as well. But I buy all my meat off Mycocks, the local Buxton butchers. I think we are quite lucky in the Peak District for the variety of food we've got – very lucky. The quality: I mean Mycocks' meat is some of the finest I've ever cooked and with me being next door, I get the pick of the meat.

How important is presentation?

Very, because people eat with their eyes. If it looks nice and it's set out nice, then you're half way there. I do traditional cooking, so no microwave, none of that sort of stuff. No ready-made sauces.

Michael Jordan, restaurant proprietor

Silver Service

The most important thing about this job is the customer and making sure they are happy with the service you are providing. However, like everything in life, some people appreciate you and some people don't, but personally I think if you're doing the best you can for people it's an enjoyable job.

58 Emma Potter and staff, The Old Hall Hotel, 2008 © Andréa Lewis

Presentation is really important. From the presentation of the food to the person that's bringing it to you – everything needs to look well presented and be cooked to a high standard. My uniform would be black shoes, black skirt and a white shirt.

In The Old Hall Hotel we're quite traditional, so silver service is something that is going a little bit out of fashion but, because we are an historic hotel, it's something people come and enjoy. We have a sweet trolley as well, where we wheel out the sweets to the table, and again, that's a fading tradition in service. A lot of new restaurants have more contemporary menus but, as I say, from the style of the hotel, lots of the customers come here because we do things in the traditional way.

Emma Potter, supervisor

Open or Wrapped?

The Elliots have run the fish and chip shop in Tideswell for three generations or more. Christine Elliot's memories go back to the early fifties and the end of rationing. The business dates back to a time when the Cressbrook and Litton Mills were going concerns...

These are memories what my mother told me. All they sold then would be fish, chips and frizalettes, which is potato dipped in batter. Some people call them scallops, fritters, dabs. They call them dabs in Lancashire but everybody liked a frizalette, from the time my mother's grandmother started the business. They came from Stockport to Tideswell – how I do not know – it was when the mills were running – which would be Cressbrook Mill and Litton Mill – and they used to do this cooking and take them down to the mill. How they got down there I do

59 Christine and David Elliot, Tideswell Chippy, 2008 © Peter Miles

not know, because there wouldn't be cars, buses or whatever. Whether they walked? More than likely, about three mile, in a basket, and people'd have them in sandwiches – butties as they'd be called then – and eat them cold 'cause they wouldn't be hot by the time they got down there.

That's how they really started, in the original shop which was in a private house next door. The front room was the chip shop and then they used to buy their chips in there and move into the other part to eat them. Then as time went on, me mother got married – she lost her grandma – and it passed to Bill, her dad, so my mother helped him. There was another brother. They fell out, why I don't know. Me mother's dad sold the original place because it was still really like a private house, and bought next door. It was all tip-top new modern stuff – gas – electric – and they kept it for many many years till her dad passed away, which left my mum and dad to do it, and they kept it for a number of years till ill-health forced him to think 'Well I can't do it any longer.' We thought it was an opportunity, me and my husband, so we had a go and we've been in it thirty years. And at the time I said to him, and I'll always remember this: 'I'll give it five years, David, and after that I'm off.' We're into our thirty-first year now!

Can you remember how things were done in your parents' time?
The fish came to Miller's Dale Station, which is long gone now, and a lorry from somewhere picked it up and dropped it outside the shop door. It was left there, nobody pinched it, nobody moved it, and it was there in a wooden box. You wouldn't do that today.

What if the weather was hot?
It was early morning actually. It came on an overnight train three times a week. Large wooden boxes and you had to have a claw hammer to take the nails out. They don't do that nowadays – they're all in polystyrene – but I do remember that.

It was a long day, I can see me mother now.... In the morning they used to prepare the potatoes and have them delivered in High Street – that's where they lived. They was rumble-cleaned in a machine full of water: all the skins, eyes, all the little blemishes taken out. Then you'd have to take them potatoes in a barrow thirty, forty yards through the Pot Market up Commercial Road to the shop which is opposite Tideswell Church, where they were put in water, ready to be chipped with a hand chipper, which then you had all sorts of shaped chips – long chips, short chips, fat chips – because you could because how you put them in the chipper was how they came out straight into the fryer. Today it's all done on the premises with an electric machine that cuts out all that heavy lifting work, but you haven't got the varied size in nice chips now. I don't think the potatoes are as good as they were then, but I might be biased.

They all have to go straight into the fryer, once they're chipped they're into the fryer. Ours is gas and electric. In mother and grandfather's day it was the coal, done by coal. There weren't gas, so they used to feed it – a little bit like trains – now they're all electric trains – there were a little door, you used to get a little shovel and the more coal you put on the hotter your fat went.

Is your batter mix a family recipe?

I'm afraid it is, and there's only two people what know, I'm one and the other's dead! So it's something what'll always pass on and probably after we're not here it'll go – but who knows?

Mind, we've got a vaster menu, as you might say. I mean, they only had fish, chips and frizalettes – didn't even have peas – that was introduced many many years after – and now we have a full, more or less a full, range: pies, sausages – both home-made - pizzas, curry sauces. Curry sauces sixty years ago? Vegetarian options, you need a microwave for quickness. As many items on the menu as food and hygiene certificates and licences on the wall!

Opening hours are different: longer hours, trades people eat different. One time there used to be a set tea-time. Nobody had tea after five o'clock, now they're eating at nine. People work shifts, people go out more, them what can't cook use it – things have changed vastly really to what it was. You pick your time when you're most needed.

Are there any special times, like harvest?

Yes, you'll get 'em now, same as lambing time, they're too busy to prepare any-thing at home. And then there's hay-making, silaging, if they're busy calving. You have set patterns of business - well-dressings or anything that brings trade in. People drive out. They like their rides to the countryside nowadays and take full advantage and call for chips – very enjoyable. We've people from Ashford, Bakewell, even Curbar – Wheston, Peak Forest, even as far as Whaley Bridge. We get quite a range of customers who bring quite a lot of trade. I wouldn't say they're farmers, but a lot of people from Chesterfield side. We're quite popular. In 1986 we was awarded the Egon Ronay Good Food Guide. Interviewed with Radio Sheffield who came out to the shop and asked us all about different things we used, what we did, how we worked and we found it a very good honour – to accept the award. Plenty of pictures in' papers – and we've kept them to this day. Now whether it'll pass through again to another generation, it's a bit doubtful.

Aren't your children interested?

No, Elizabeth has got her own life and career and my son, he farms 'cause we live on a farm as well, so we've always had a busy life, but who knows? I didn't think I'd ever go in it – never – never – so who knows what lies round the corner or what door opens? – Which we don't. Nobody knows.

Table

Food and drink are social currency. We learn to talk at the table, which becomes a microcosm of the fields where the food we cook and eat comes from. We may grow our own in gardens (page 102), or allotments (page 103), where accomplished social skills such as chatting or courtship are developed. Taken overall, there are half-a-dozen marriages made through food in this book.

People gather at the table. Be it for mealtimes in the home, or special occasions such as Christmas, Fairs and Wakes (page 109) where whole communities come together to celebrate themselves. Which is why they're included in this section; a village's social table can be as great as its water table, and may well date back to at least pagan times. It is a natural system of stretching resources by salting, preserving and brewing, be it pork and bacon (page 124), vegetables (page 122), fruit and jam (page 122), beers and wines (page 122), it becomes a means to lay on extra, to put the feast in festival. This bringing-together, sharing of resources and effort, is typified by the Derbyshire tradition of a fuddle (page 110). A failure to identify small scale rural cohesion may lead to a widening gap between locals and visitors, between young and old as Russell Ashfield and Sue Jackson fear (page 130). Yet it's clear that items like Taddington Tea Bread help to bring and keep communities together; this is evident in another sense when Christine Gregory says, "I think, as I mentioned to you before, it doesn't really belong to me, the recipe."

Nothing is wasted, not even sheep's heads (page 121). Rationing – which extended to the mid-fifties – elevated the skills of making the most at the table to a premium. It also meant an urban population were encouraged to grow and keep items they might expect to buy, and Land Army recruits had to learn a very different way of life, as Jean Brocklehurst recalls (page 113). Food was used for remedies (page 126) if of doubtful medical efficacy, but part of a wholesome healthy life-style.

To throw food away was unthinkable, whereas today, where we have refrigerators and freezers to help defer decay, over a fifth of what we buy ends up in the bin, uneaten. Perhaps the microwave makes its too easy. Despite – or because of – TV celebrity chefs, following a recipe and going beyond ping-food (the microwave) has become a journey into the unknown. Simple pleasures of making and eating home-made bread and jam are close to becoming extinct rather than a commonplace, just as damsons, which Jill Horton picks (page 122), and which make the finest jam in the world, are otherwise virtually unobtainable. In the supermarket, there seems a huge amount of choice, but precious little natural variety. Not even "This is not just any food, this is M and S food" is ever quite the same as the real

Table 101

thing which family and friends share in the making as well as the eating.

As Ian Lawton and Will Oven put it:

"It's very simple. You eat something at its best when it's ripe and it's only ripe once a year. We're having all these things artificially done out of season and that's where the flavour went. The other thing is the freshness. The freshest it can be in a supermarket is at least forty-eight hours old – it doesn't matter how many times you run up and down the motorway." (page 105)

"You don't eat the same food as you used to. It isn't as fresh as what it used to be. Fresh food it used to be before and now it isn't. It's all manufactured." (page 88)

If you have any special recipes you'd like to share with others, or want to cook some of the dishes mentioned in this book, visit:

http://thefarminglifecentre.org.uk/seasons_to_taste.

Milking by Hand

According to a story that was how my mum and dad got together.... My mum came from a little village in Ireland. She came over like a lot of people did in the late thirties/early forties and she came to work on a farm down the road from where my father lived. She and her sister were coming up on bikes one day and my dad thought, "Oh, they look alright, I'll chat them up." Me dad says to me mum, "I bet you can't milk a cow."

"I bet I can."

"I bet you can't."

"I bet I can."

He didn't know where she was from or anything about her and so he says, "I'll find you a cow to milk."

"I'll be up tonight at milking time and I'll show you."

He found her a heifer that had not been long calved, with very, very little teats.

"There you are, there's your heifer, there's your bucket, there's your stool, sit down and milk it."

And my mum came along sat under this cow and she milked every drop off, every single drop, so that was the start of the romance and that's why I'm here today.

Pauline Jackson, milk lady

Growing vegetables

We'd a big vegetable patch; we grew potatoes, more or less enough to keep us through the winter and carrots too. Since we've been married I had a plot down at farm and used to grow everything, enough for the three households. Carrots, potatoes, peas, cabbage, cauliflowers – you name it. I can't do it now.

William Mycock, farmer

He misses it a lot but he just can't do it. Mind you he's eighty-four – he was eighty-four last week, so you can't expect a lot!

Margaret Mycock, farmer's wife

There're pea rows in the garden. We always have them because we really like peas, and we've got loads of photos of when I'm little sitting in the pea rows with my toy, my teddy bear and a dog, and I'm eating peas straight off the bush. They're really nice, they taste great.

Erica Jackson, fourteen year old daughter of Sue Jackson

A Garden from Bakewell to Breadsall

I was a railway man and I was at Rowsley at one time and there was quite a lot of railway men had gardens, allotments at Rowsley and when I got transferred to

Table   103

Derby the same thing happened there. I've come to the conclusion that due to the rotten shifts as we used to have in them days, there wasn't the social life that anybody who had a nine-to-five job could have and you had to make your own hobbies. Not only was gardening a good exercise hobby, but also put some food on the table at the same time. That's why, I think, in most railway centres there seems to be a lot of gardens for staff and allotments. At Derby we used to have a garden shop. You could buy fertiliser and different things for the garden. I was reading some time ago in a gardening book, the big demand there is for allotments now. It said there was upwards of two million on the waiting list.

60 Margaret Oven, farming wife, still grows her own vegetables today, 2008
© Damian Hughes

The Headmaster we'd got at Middleton, he fair drilled gardening into you. When you came into Standard 4, I think you'd be about twelve or so, you used to have a little plot. It was about as big as this room. And we used to have geometrical drawing on a Friday. One of the things we always had to draw was where we were setting us crops for the next year. We used to draw it all and rotate it so the same crop wasn't grown in the same place above once every four years. You'd not grow potatoes in the same place for the next three years. Same with greens and things like that. We rotated because of the diseases in the ground or taking nutrients out. As you rotate it you get better crops. That was the idea of it. Headmaster used to insist on it. Only boys had the plots. All of them got a turn at it before they left school. Some liked it and some didn't. You couldn't choose anything. You were told. We provided seed and we took crops home.

The last allotment as I had anything to do with was on the Cromford Road about twenty years ago. I grew all sorts: potatoes, cabbage, kidney beans, broad beans, all sorts of things like that, and blackcurrants, gooseberries and apples. Oh, there's different ideas come up. Some are good, some aren't. But it's still the same, a good digging, good depth of soil, plenty of muck and that's gardening.

Oh, yes, that's another thing you see. You couldn't compost enough to keep a garden going. It goes down to so small an amount. When it's died down there's not a great lot from a bin-full. The farmer used to bring a load of muck and chuck it over the fence and it was there when you wanted it, in a heap. Nowadays you never seem to have any heaps. Poultry manure I've been putting on recently. I've

61 Bakewell allotments, 2008 © David Fine

found that very, very good. I usually get it from Wilco's at Matlock, in boxes.

Those allotments as we had on Cromford Road were quite big. They were four shillings a year. I think it were about half a crown at Middleton and those at Grammar School were about the same. That would be up till early sixties when they extended the school and we lost us gardens. Same as we lost them on Cromford Road when the houses were built.

There were no rules. You were expected to keep' paths tidy. There were some of them that didn't used to bother about the paths and we used to get on to 'em, tell 'em to get their fingers out and get cracking and they used to do it. Some used to sell extra crops. I used to give ours away. I can always say I've never sold anything out of a garden. You could always find somebody to have it.

Oh yeah, we had shows. When I was a very young kid they used to have an annual show at Middleton and some years later, about late forties, early fifties we built a new Institute, in us spare time. To get money to run it I suggested we run the old show again. We organised this show and ran it for several years. The profit went to' Institute like. A lot of stuff was left and it was auctioned off at night to increase funds. Eventually they had one at Wirksworth. They used to have it in the Red Lion, in the club room. The one they had at Wirksworth, I shall never forget.

I was having a drink at' bar one night and a chap came down. His face was red as anything. I thought, "What's he been up to now?" Because he was a chap who fetched stuff in from other places. Go and beg it off someone to show if it were good, or buy it to show. He had to win.

Table   105

"Eh, I'm glad to see thee," he says.

"Why?"

He says, "You know those eggs I've got in' show?"

"Well, you've got two lots, them brown 'uns and white 'uns."

"Aye, brown 'uns as I'm on about. They want to know what sort of birds as laid 'em."

"Didn't you tell 'em?"

"I don't know."

"Brown eggs have been laid with brown Leghorns."

"Oh, thank you," he says. And off he went upstairs again. There was such a noise upstairs and he come down after a while.

"You've done me, you bugger," he says.

"Why?"

"They've never been laid by a brown hen. A brown hen lays a white egg."

"Aye," I says, "But it's time you were stopped at this game."

"Aye, they banned me. What sort were they?"

"They were Well Summers." That's what they was that laid them; beautiful brown eggs. Lemon meringues and all they used to make. And they used to like to get them for shows. But there were very few folks kept them. We kept fowls, we had some Well Summers but we never showed the eggs. They were beautiful birds an' all. But he never did it no more. He were banned all around for that. And he were our secretary at Middleton show. That's what nettled me about it. But my mate as worked with me said "His garden goes from Bakewell to Breadsall."

Hubert Doxey, railwayman

Everybody Talks About Where The Flavour Went

It's very simple. You eat something at its best when it's ripe and it's only ripe once a year. We're having all these things artificially done out of season and that's where the flavour went. The other thing is the freshness. The freshest it can be in a supermarket is at least forty-eight hours old – it doesn't matter how many times you run up and down the motorway. Pick some peas or dig some potatoes up from the garden. Boil them and eat them and then, people say they can't understand, but that's where the flavour went. It's the reluctance to prepare it in the home, number one and number two it's the length of the supply chain.

We were seasonal eaters so there was something exciting to come, from a food point of view, throughout the year. Who wants strawberries on Christmas Day, what nonsense is that? Wimbledon's the time to eat strawberries. If you eat things in season, that's when you get the flavour.

Ian Lawton, livestock auctioneer

Farm fresh

You don't eat the same food as you used to. It isn't as fresh as what it used to be. Fresh food it used to be before and now it isn't. It's all manufactured.

Wilf Oven, farmer

Range cooking

It was pretty basic, you had to cook what you could get. We only had the fire, so we had food cooked in a big pan behind the fire with soot and God knows what that got in it all the time. That was the only cooking we had, otherwise you used the oven and let things go in it all day, and because the oven was at the side of the range, while ever you had a fire the oven kept warm. Bacon always smelled nice but it was dicey cooking bacon on the fire because you were lucky if you didn't get soot all over it. I never remember us being without food ever, there always was food, but it was bread and jam, bread and dripping, that sort of thing. Mum used to make all the bread, she was not so accurate with her measurements so sometimes it was good and sometimes it was not so good. Mother often baked on Friday and she got the bread ready first and then she would cook pastry because it was hot – scones and jam tarts or fruit pies if fruit was available and

62 Range cooking – an old range adapted for modern use, 2006
© Alison Furness, Courtesy of the photographer and REAP

Table   107

she would do meat and potato pies. Then she cooked cake because the oven wanted to be slower for cake and then the bread went in after this when it had risen on the chair in front of the fire and that lasted you through until the next Friday, hopefully. There was no question of disliking food – "Don't be so daft, get it down ya!" Food was not to be wasted.

Joan Stewartson, housewife

Milking Machines

The milk used to come down this cooler and every now and again it would freeze up and the milk that was frozen on there, we used to bite it off, we used to pick it off and then bite it, suck it. It was absolutely beautiful.

Pauline Jackson, milk lady

Boiled Cabbage

My mum was a great fan of the pressure cooker, which is terrible for cabbage, it ruins it; it ruins any green vegetable. She cooked everything in the pressure cooker. Yeah, I do remember that.

Sue Jackson, farmer

Hot and Cold

You had no hot water to the sink, no bathroom, just a bath in front of the fire on a Friday night, one of those big tin baths. But you all kept clean, everywhere was spotless. No central heating, more healthy. We used to have frost on the inside of the windows, it was so cold.

My mum made all her own bread, everything. In those days they did, even though there was no cooker. It was a side oven, coal fired, and people have often said to me, "How did they get the temperature for a sponge cake in a side oven?" I suppose you had to stoke the fire up and you felt with your hand and with experience, you'd get used to it. Mum didn't have recipes and it was a shame that we never put it all down, what she used to do, because she guessed everything. And isn't it sad when the recipes go with them? She used to make beautiful caraway cakes, caraway seed bread and she never left us the recipe. When you think back, if only you'd have put these things down......

Favourites of mine? – Meat and potato pie and rabbit pie. The majority of people when I was young kept rabbits for their own use. We kept rabbits. How my mother could have killed and skinned them I don't know. We always had fish on Good Friday but it was a luxury. You didn't have tins of salmon or anything like that. That was a luxury in those days. She could make a meal on anything really, years ago. Bones, for making broth.... boiling bones from the butcher's and that, vegetables, all that type of thing. My mum made oatcakes to sell to the

*63 'It was so cold'. A bed warming
pan and stoneware hot water bottles
in place of central heating?*
© Lynne Mycock and Hannah Watson

butchers. There were butchers that came for so many dozen per week. They were
made on a flat griddle across your fire. Rub the top of it with a chunk of suet and
make the oatcakes. Everybody was on the same level in those days. You left your
door open when you went out. You knew nobody would enter. Everybody tried
to help each other really.

Puddings were different. One of the highlights of our life was when my
mother was baking bread we would have what she called barmy dumplings. They
were little pieces of dough put into boiling water for ten minutes and get them
out and they're gorgeous with treacle or jam. My nephew used to come up for
meals to my mum's as well as my two girls and when my mum had done bread
they used to fall out as to who should have these barmy dumplings, who ate the
most. On Pancake Day we would see how many pancakes we could eat with either
sugar and lemon or treacle. But all the sweets were different then because you
had the likes of jam and suet roly-poly and rice pudding and things like that that
would go in the side oven. And you had a hook on the fireplace with a pan of
water to do your suety dumplings and all that. It was very warm in that room and
up above. Everywhere else was freezing. We really needed gloves and boots on,
it was so cold. And then, of course, there were no water closets, it was in the back
yard. You had no hot water bottles. You had the oven shelf to take to bed. A shelf
out of the oven, wrap it up in a blanket and take it to bed with you. It used to
keep hot for hours, or a brick, a house brick, put it in the oven for a long while

Table   109

and then take that. No electric blankets; no electric! I don't think the young ones today can understand anything of what it must have been like.

Dorothy Prince, housewife

Brassington Wakes

One of the big things that used to happen was Brassington Wakes and my Gran, who used to live at the farm, moved into Brassington when my parents took over the farm and she always used to have a huge, great Wakes Day celebration meal. She used to do the most lovely dish and the whole family would get round her great, big table. She lived in a teeny little place and the table took the whole room up and we'd all squash in and she'd have boiled some broiler chicken, broiler hens, two or three the day before, and used to make these lovely tasty chicken dishes with a very tasty white sauce and boiled eggs and things like this. I remember she used to have this lovely great big salad. She used to grow her bits and pieces in the garden so there'd be these lovely crispy lettuces and bread from Dykes, the baker, in Hognaston which used to be lovely. And proper butter from Brindleys in the village. Used to have a great, big slab of butter where you used to cut it off and sell it by the pound ...and this chicken, you never taste chicken like that these days, it's just lovely, very, very flavoursome, lovely. So that was always special as far as we kids were concerned – and you know, I have really wonderful memories.

Jill Horton, farmer's daughter

Grindon Wakes

What great days they were. It's about run out now, but in the olden days they used to kill a couple of animals. They used to buy the animals off the farms in the village and slaughter them up at the pub. Tom Bagshaw from Butterton used to be the butchers. He'd just go around the village with his basket delivering and selling to people – twenty or thirty pound joints. The village came together at The Shoulder of Mutton in Grindon [now The Cavalier] and they'd have a big fry up one day with liver and onions. A lot of the old beer drinkers used to go for that.

Relations came. It was really a big celebration the Wakes. There's quite a lot of villages still run it but not on the same scale as they did then. Same as Longnor and Hartington Wakes. But nothing like it used to be. I'll always remember Grindon wakes 'cause I was living in Grindon. We looked forward to it.

They had plum puddings in them days, like Christmas puddings, but home-made – with brandy sauce. Some people had frummety[3], but I never did. Oh it was

---

3 Furmety. The drink in Hardy's *The Mayor of Casterbridge*. Also Furmity was a kind of porridge prepared in various parts of Britain from wheat, water, milk, fruit and eggs, often consumed after sheep-shearing.

quite a get together wakes was. Then your harvest festival came on after that. Everyone would go to church and everybody sent something in – your produce. They used to sell it and the proceeds went back to the church then. We enjoyed it then. That was what we looked forward to, you know, wakes, bank holidays and Easter – not that you got bank holidays off on a farm, because you had to be there seven days a week.

Bill Chadwick, farmer

Hope and Hathersage Fairs

One of my earliest recollections was Hathersage Fair in October. They brought all these young horses down and the cattle and put them in our field and they separated them because those that were going over to Stannington side went up the old dale at Hathersage and those that were going to Holmesfield went over by Fox House. So they separated these young horses 'cause they could run. It was like a rodeo in those days and of course we weren't allowed out, we just had to look from the bedroom window, but it was quite exciting to see it going on.

Farmers sold their own or they bartered. Hope Fair, Hathersage Fair, and then they had sheep sales at Yorkshire Bridge, Marquis and various things in the autumn when farmers, particularly on the hills, they'd got an excess of lambs, they couldn't winter 'cause it was a hard winter, and they would sell them on – what we call stores. They would stand at the side of the road with them and the dog would keep them in the pen and eventually they would bargain for whatever price.

There was a chappie at Hope, he was a dealer and he'd sell anything. Said he'd sell the missus if anybody'd give him a good price! It was on a Saturday this particular year because it was always on the 13th May and a chap bought some lambs down from Edale and they got within a penny for the price of these lambs and neither of them would budge so they adjourned to The Old Hall, and drunk this penny many times. When they came out the chap from Hope said "You'll not get them home before dark so you'd better put them in my field." When he came for them on Sunday morning he said "I think we'd better split that penny seeing as you had them in my field all night." The other man replied "I never do business on a Sunday," walked them back to Edale, where the Hope man went on the Monday, bought them and brought them back again!

Ray Platts, farmer

A Befuddled Fuddle

Just after the war we all said we'd take something to work, when I was on munitions. Some took food and I said, "I can bring a bottle of wine."

"Oh, lovely," they said.

Well, we all went home merry! I can't remember if it was wheat or potato wine

Table   111

but it was twenty-odd years old so you can imagine... We called these do's a fuddle, a very old term when everyone brought something to the table. Some people had brought what food they could get, but, you see, everything was rationed, sweets and everything was rationed, but I'd taken this wine.

Dorothy Prince, housewife

Mother's Meals

Me mother used to like to run the shop, organise it you know, buy all the produce and that 'cause she liked doing that. Quite happy to let her do that, I used to play a minor part in it as well. *She used to do bed and breakfast, take all the old soldiers in.* When the war was on, just after the war as well, she had the kindergarten children coming for dinner each day. They used to be down the avenue at Dr Watson's old house in Bakewell and she used to have about up to thirty children for dinner every day. I still meet them now and they're grown up but still say "Your mother's meals were marvellous." Still can taste the treacle tarts and apple tarts what she used to make for your dinner. She used to do all the baking herself. *Me mother's treacle tarts were out of this world. You'll never get one like me mother's.* And she used to run the shop and cook the meals at the same time. *She used to get up at 5 o'clock in the morning and get the coal fire going.* She used to cook the meals on the side. *She used to get up and scrub all the shop floor 'cause it was stone floor and that takes some doing that.* She used to donkeystone the shop doorway, that's a whitening stone to do the edge of the door, the doorstep. You never see donkeystone nowadays though do you? *And then she had a grate in the house and she used to put black lead on it, colour it with black stuff.* Everything was spotless. She was very well liked, everybody thought the world of me mother in Bakewell. They did really.

Graham and Michael Skidmore, greengrocers, Bakewell

Land Army

The uniform was lovely. It really was lovely. Corduroy knee breaches, laced at the side, from down the leg up to the knee, and lovely fine corduroy fabric. Then we had a fawn, stone-coloured shirt, and a bottle green tie, with long stockings, up to the knee, then turned over in khaki colour. Then the most wonderful khaki overcoat, cloth like the officers wore in the army, and lovely brown brogue shoes, lovely quality. We had wellingtons, and overalls in khaki, and bib and brace to work in. The uniform itself for best wear, it was most smart, and a little pork pie hat, which, eventually, I wore working on the farm. You think, well, you're not going to want them again, and you keep them and treasure them, and treasure them, and then you think, "If I was going on the tractor nearly all day, might as well have something warm on and..." Yes, we had a lovely uniform.

I was the youngest of four that came, and for some reason, I don't know why, I was always allocated to do the speaking for the four of us. The next morning we were taken from the War Agriculture Office in Bakewell to a farm at the top of the thirteen bends. The farm manager took us into the field. He knew that we were newcomers to the Land Army but he never showed us what to do at all. Gave us all a hoe, put us in a damn great field that looked twenty miles long, with furrows, and said do these, chop these all out. Of course having not seen plants before to know what they were, we left all the good strong standing ones up, and chopped all the others out. We'd thought we'd done a jolly good job. That night, when this man came up with one of the lorries from the Express Dairies, and he got out of it, and came across to see how we'd done, and said, "What the hell have you lot been doing?"

64 Jean Brocklehurst,
Land Army Girl, 1943
© Courtesy Tom Brocklehurst

We thought we'd made a super job. Well we had. We'd chopped all the things out that should have been left in, and left all the weeds behind. We weren't very popular!

He was very, very cross.

"Oh my goodness," I said, "We weren't to know. Why didn't they tell us what to do?"

He said I was rude to answer him back. I was dismissed straight away, I got the chop. The other three girls were so upset for me, because as I say, they always let me do the speaking. The next morning I had to go report to the War Agriculture Office. Mr. Wells, who was the boss of the War Ag., he questioned me and I told him the truth.

"Well, in that case," he said, "I'll ring Mr. Moseley up." which he did, and they said I could go back and join the others. I arrived at the farm to start work again in a shining limousine. A few days later I was in Bakewell and spotted this Mr. Moseley across the road, so I thought, well I'd better go across to him and tell

Table 113

him what actually happened.

How I came to meet Tom was the day we joined the Land Army. We went to the Agriculture Office to sign in, we four girls, and struggled down the stairs with all our cases piled up, stood there getting our breath back and having a little chat, when this young man came through, and said, "Would you excuse me, ladies?"

Later I said to these girls, "Well, if they're all as polite as him, he'll do." because it was one thing my parents made us heed, above anything else that mattered more in life, practically than anything, kind ways and good manners; and how true they were.

Never thought any more about it till we went to his farm. He come asking for extra Land Girls, because his father was ill with peritonitis, very ill and he was running the farm and it was potato planting time, and they wanted a gang of girls to go potato planting. But none of us had potato planted before, but I was delighted to go. Tom says some were six inches, and some were twelve, and you got to guess what the others were, they were all over the place. Tom started to go out with me, and we were courting for four and a half years, till we were married. But when we went up to his farm, that day, I thought 'Oh my God, it's the last place God made.' never thinking I'd live up there, ten or eleven years. And yet when it's your home it's totally different. It had the most wonderful views, all the villages around we could see from the front of the cottage.

Jean Brocklehurst, farmer's wife

Rationing

Everything was rationed. When I was working at Burnets we were only allowed two or three ounces of butter and about four ounces of cheese but with heavy work on a farm I think we got a bit extra – a lot of people could make their own butter and cheese in them days, so it didn't make too much difference really. We didn't bother telling the authorities. Many used to kill pigs...mind you, you had to register if you had any pigs, and when you killed a pig they knocked so much off your rations. In them days everybody prepared for hard winters and you stored stuff up, your flour and oatmeal. They had their own hens and eggs and plenty of milk.

Bill Chadwick, farmer

During the war we had our regular customers who were registered with us and they could get their main provisions – seven of them: butter, bacon, lard, margarine, sugar and tea. That's only six so there must have been another one – cheese. They were the seven rations we kept and we were allowed to buy enough for our customers that were registered with us. If we could get a bit extra, well, that was under the counter and it was quite profitable and possibly our rations helped to eke that out. My mother was a bit unscrupulous, but there wasn't much spare, nobody could get much spare. As regards to tin goods and sweets, they were on coupons. You had a ration book with so many coupons and they changed the value of these coupons periodically. There were As, Bs, and Cs. As were worth one point, Bs two and Cs four and if there was more stuff from the government they put the value of the points up or down, but that covered tin goods and jam and stuff like that, not perishable goods. Sweets were Ds and Es and, again, Ds would be worth perhaps one point and Es two points. Depending on how things were, if you had four Ds you would perhaps be able to have four ounces of sweets or a bar of chocolate.

Joan Stewartson, housewife

Black Market

The Ministry of Food took everything. People said we had guaranteed prices but we could have made far more of the food if we could have sold it ourselves. But you had to sell it to the Ministry of Food and that was why there was a black market. I can remember standing and talking to a chap in Bakewell Market and a fella came up to him and said "How much do I owe you?"

It was forty-five pounds and this fella took out a wad of notes and counted out forty five pounds into his hand and then said "Thank you very much." and off he went.

When he'd gone this chap said, "It was a ham I had to spare - I meant the weight of it." ...so it was a pound a pound! In those days it would probably have been three shillings!

Ray Platts, farmer

School Dinners from the Fifties – Hardwick Square Junior School, Buxton

I was absolutely petrified when I started because one of the ladies was my mum's age and I'd always called her Mrs Marshall, and of course she said call her Gwen and I couldn't...Yes I was scared of dropping things because they were all heavy, yes it was very frightening. But the children were quite funny especially the little ones - they used to come up and they didn't know quite what they were supposed to do and they used to stand there and you had to kind of say, "Well come on now, you can have this, that and the other," And they used to stand there and say, "Well, I'm not quite sure what I would like."

And then you'd have to kind of push them along a bit.

It was no use trying to make them eat everything because they wouldn't. I mean everybody tried. If it were chips...yes, but otherwise it was a struggle. Cabbage! They hated that the most. Ravioli was just coming in then, they didn't like that - and soya meat, a kind of imitation meat. They didn't like that at all.

Table   115

The left-over food went into big bins and the pig swill man eventually fetched it from Silverlands.

Main courses? There was stew and dumplings, sausages, pilchards, beef, pork and lamb. Mince, meat pie, luncheon meat which was served with a salad, cheese which was served with a salad, cheese pie, fish fingers, ravioli, cod and soya. Did I say lamb? I've forgotten. Lamb.

Then the veg was cauliflower, mushy peas, carrots, swedes, onions and brussels at Christmas and cabbage and what else have I got...salads. When we had a salad they had raw carrot, lettuce, egg, cress, tomato and celery. Potatoes – they were either mashed, boiled, sauté, chips, home made crisps or roast – we didn't very often have roasts. And sauces – they had cheese, mint sauce, onion sauce, parsley and mayonnaise.

Now the puddings. There was Manchester tart, apple pie and custard, prunes and custard, sponge pudding and custard, coconut pudding and custard, apple-upside-down cake and custard, stewed apple, spotted dick, home made biscuits, ice cream... But I can't remember what they had with the ice cream. Rice pudding and semolina and jam.

So that's it. I think they had a very, very good menu.

Margaret Coleman, school dinner lady

Taddington Fruit Bread

I think, as I mentioned to you before, it doesn't really belong to me, the recipe. It's a lady that lives only a very short distance away from here, Anne Andrews. I understand it was her mother's recipe and her mum lived on Tideswell Moor just beyond Peak Forest.

One year we had a fair for the children down at Taddington Hall and we had all sorts of things. The children ran races on the lawns. We had a raffle and Anne Andrews sat in the garage down at the bottom of the yard with a table and two lovely big Taddington Fruit Breads in roasting tins. One of them, she was cutting up and buttering for people to taste and selling raffle tickets for the other one, so we all bought a raffle ticket with the recipe attached to it. I can't remember who won, but, of course, from then on people were manufacturing Taddington Fruit Bread in the village wholesale. Any church event or any school sale of home-made cakes or anything, there was Taddington Fruit Bread. It's a bit like the Women's Institute and the Victoria Sandwich recipe; they give them all the same ingredients and when they arrive at the competition they're all different and Taddington Fruit Bread's just the same!

People still make it now. The recipe Anne gave us just makes the one roasting tin. My daughter worked down in Bakewell at Cheese Etc. which was a deli-catessen. They baked on the premises and she told John, the owner, about

65 Taddington Fruit Bread, 2008 © Hannah Watson

Taddington Fruit Bread.

"Would you like to bring me a piece, I might be able to sell it."

She took a piece down and he tasted it. "Oh yes, yes. Well now, is your Mum going to make it or shall I?"

"I don't think she'll give you the recipe."

I didn't, and that's how it all started. It just grew and grew and grew until I could hardly cope. I'd make a batch... I'd do a roasting tin and cut it up into about twelve pieces, but then I started baking them individually in small and large cakes and she would take forty or fifty at a time and perhaps that would be twice a week. Then there was another chap who used to call in at the delicatessen and he used to have a market stall at Chelford and Bakewell. Sally being Sally, she told him all about it and he used to come every Friday night at about five o'clock and he'd have about ninety a week.

Christine Gregory, farmer's wife

Cooking for the family

I've made oatcakes right up until recently. It's just a bit of a mixture of oatmeal, flour, bit of salt and a bit of yeast, made up into a sort of batter. And I'd always do them on a frying pan like a pancake. I use to make quite a stack – they'd last

Table   117

more or less up to a week and nowadays you could freeze them. I've just made four Christmas cakes this time, one each for the girls and one for a friend and I usually make them a Christmas pudding. I've got a recipe that I was given before I was married, it was Aunty Gladys's, she would have been a hundred by now and it was her mother's and I still use it. Lynne, my daughter-in-law, likes them – her dad did too, he was very fond of them. They have Guinness in as well as milk, suet, flour, eggs and fruit. I sometimes wonder if they're worth making but I've got this cooker going regular. It's not like having to put electric on every time because it's a long process boiling them.

Margaret Mycock, farmer's wife

66 Aunty Gladys's Mother's Christmas Pudding with Margaret Mycock, 2008 © Lynne Mycock

Oatcakes, puddings and ducks

There were always cakes on the go, baking. I still do make oatcakes. The recipe was given to me by an elderly lady in the village because she used to make oatcakes and sell them for the church. Now I make them and sell them at church fairs here.

They do vary. I suppose I make perhaps a little bit thicker than some. I know some that you buy in the shops are very thin. With all these things, you add things, you take things away or you make it a bit different. I make half and half, half oatmeal and half strong white flour, just yeast and a bit of salt. I don't put as much salt in now as I used to do but I do put salt in because it doesn't seem right if you don't. I make a pound and a half of each. So, that's three pound of dry and then put an ounce of yeast to it.

67 Griddle pans for oatcakes, 2008 © Damian Hughes

I always use fresh yeast which I get locally, Taylor's Mill down in South Wingfield. It's what you get used to. I always did use the fresh yeast which, you could get it in Buxton but then they stopped doing it. It comes in the blocks down here at the mill. It comes in a square block. I don't know what amount there'd be in it, two pounds possibly.

I know the lady said one day when I was there, "We used to have ten blocks delivered and it would be gone before the end of the week. It used to come on a Tuesday and people were waiting for it to come fresh in. But now, sometimes, we don't get through it at all."

So they don't have as much delivered now. Instead they have the bread makers and use the dried yeast, you see. But I never got on well with the dried yeast. I have made the oatcakes with the dried yeast but it doesn't rise the same.

The same as with the oatmeal puddings... well, known as oatmeal puddings... the black pudding. I think Mother's got it in her recipe book there. It says oatmeal blood pudding, I think that's how she's written it but I know what it is. She's written my oatcake recipe down there.

Margaret Oven, farmer's wife

Beastings

In those days, when you'd the cow calved, everybody wanted the first milking from the cow. It was called beasting, or colostrum as it's known today, and they made beasting custard. It was so very rich you'd just make custard and put a crust on it. You'd let the calf have some, but what was left over... It was quite a quite a thing, people just went mad for the first or second milkings of the cow. It was an old wives' tale that you didn't wash the utensil you'd taken the milk in, they gave it back dirty.

Thomas Maltby, farmer

Table 119

Junket

They were pretty good at utilising some of the parts of animals that we would now consider as not really worth using. One thing I can think of is junket, which was made from milk. You used a thing called rennet, which comes from a calf's stomach, which made a semi-liquid type milk pudding called junket. I don't think many people would be thinking about using something which comes from a calf's stomach now.

Tony Kemish, farmer

Milk Surplus

We went out of milk-selling in about 1970 and of course, you've got the cows there so obviously you've got surplus on hand after feeding the calves. I started making butter and cheese, just to use the milk, not to sell or anything. That was through the help of Auntie Nellie. Brian's mother had got a little glass butter churn. We had a big, end-over-end butter churn but it hadn't been used for years and was in the loft. Anyway, we didn't fancy it so I used to make it in this... it was only a gallon, you could only fill it half full, which I did and made butter and, of course, salted it down again in stone jars... packing. You put layers of salt in between and then you just wash the salt out when you come to use it. That's what they always did, you see, so they'd got it for the winter time. There were no freezers.

"Well, I haven't got rennet."

"Well, we can get rennet."

So, I go to the chemist for rennet but, of course, it's only the junket rennet. It's not quite as strong. Auntie Nellie said, "I think I might have a bottle that was my mother's."

It was many years old. It still had the label and she said, "I remember mother making it. We'll carry on from there."

If you let milk go off, sour, you can make curd cheese, can't you? Then we improvised with cake tins as the moulds and used muslin to put the curds in; made holes in the bottom of the cake tins so it would drain. You put the curds in and the whey drained off

68 Traditional butter churns, 2008
© Damian Hughes

69 Glass butter churns and an electric cream separator, 2008 © Damian Hughes

and it was similar to a cross between a Cheshire and Cheddar which was quite nice, really. Different people that tried it liked it. We didn't sell it, obviously, it was only for ourselves, but it takes quite a quantity to do. We could feed the whey to the pigs, 'cause we'd a few pigs at the time.

Margaret Oven, farmer's wife

Posset

Most people made their own bread and they'd only bake usually, once a week. The bread got a little bit stale but, by putting the milk and raisins in it and cooking it, it didn't lose its flavour. They cooked cheese and milk, and you cooked cheese in with the milk. Then they used to make what was known as posset, that was milk with so much beer, and drink that. And you'd have it at night, particularly in winter. There was far, far more milk used then per household than ever there is today, because the milk's only put in tea and coffee today. There's very few milk puddings and things like that.

Thomas Maltby, farmer

Hasty Pud

There's quite a bit of guesswork in some of my family's old recipes, you don't have specific weights and measures. Some of the sponge cake and all-in-one type recipes are ones that have been used in the family a long time. There's one recipe which isn't written down anywhere, which my mother used to do when there was a panic and everybody wanted to have something to eat and something sweet and nice. And she used to call it hasty pud and it was wonderful. You used to get a big pan of boiling milk, while it was boiling you used to sprinkle in ordinary flour and it used to thicken and go all gloopy and gorgeous and then it was

Table   121

spooned out into a dish and you'd either have treacle on it or you'd have sugar and butter on it and it was delicious and I remember that as being one of my favourites. It was really, really lovely and I've asked lots and lots of people about it and nobody's ever heard of it.

Lots of recipes, lots of things have been passed down. My grandmother was a lovely cook and I used to watch her cooking Sunday lunch and lots of little things that she used to do are things that I do automatically really. It's like using the cheapest cuts of meats and using the things that perhaps aren't terribly popular but, you know, make lovely, lovely dishes and I think my kids have benefited from that and it certainly makes for good, interesting food.

Jill Horton, farmer's daughter

Brawn

I used to do the brawn, I never made black pudding or sausages but I used to make brawn. It's very simple really, because you cook whatever you want – pieces of face or whatever you want to use and put a pig's trotter or two to get the setting of it, take it out and take the meat off any bones and mince it up and season it with sage, pepper and salt and mix liquid in to what you think is the consistency to set and leave it in basins to gel.

Margaret Mycock, farmer's wife

Let nowt go to waste

We used to cook a sheep's head and make it into a sort of meat paste. It would see you through the week. That was the old saying. "As long as it's got its eyes it will see you through the week!"

I couldn't bear taking eyes out. I'd have a sheep's head but I didn't want the eyes left in. There's quite a lot of meat though, I know, heads and tongues. I mean, people squirm at it, but I sometimes used to take the tongue out and salt it. I'm quite fond of a tongue. Beef-tongue, it's sealed now, vacuum packed. I still salt it and it eats quite nicely. It's different, I think, when you do it yourself. Savoury ducks, oatmeal blood puddings, yes, a quart of fresh pig's blood which Mother did use. I still do make savoury ducks and they all go; family like them.

Margaret Oven, farmer's wife

PYO

An apple tree, yes, and there were damsons in the hedgerows. We did a lot of blackberrying... and mushrooms, going in the fields for mushrooms. My mother used to make blackberry vinegar and that was good for coughs and colds during the winter. You put a tablespoon or two in a cup with boiling water. It warmed you up as well as curing the cough and the cold. You get your blackberries, wash them and then put so much sugar on them and leave them for a few days, keep turning them. Then sieve them and add your vinegar and bottle it. A lot of times we would have Yorkshire Pudding on its own as a pudding with raspberry or blackberry vinegar on it instead of treacle. And you did your Kilner jars. You did all your own fruit, bottled it.

70 Elderflower, one of many pick your own crops, Bridge 2008
© Damian Hughes

Dorothy Prince, housewife

As a family we always used to rely on what was growing around. We always used to go picking blackberries. We used to pick crab apples that were in the trees and hedges locally. We always used to pick sloes and make sloe gin for Christmas, that was a must. Watercress was another thing, we always used to go down the Bradbourne Brook and pick watercress, that was a Sunday afternoon walk, we'd go as a family and pick watercress and bring that back. We do collect blackberries still. We do make our blackberry jam, I do pick my damsons and make my chutneys and jellies, all those sorts of things. It's part of how we live our lives and it's very important to me.

Jill Horton, farmer's daughter

Fermentation

You made your own beer when you were threshing, hay-making. You made you own beer with nettles and that sticky stuff. Nettles, dandelion with a bottle of Mason's Extract from the chemist. You added that to it with yeast. You had to leave it and then skim it off. ...and, when it was ready, beautiful! Of course it all had to be sieved and I remember we were still making it when my youngest daughter was little and I think we were up the garden or something and she and her friend were in. She'd only be about ten or eleven and she said a bomb had gone off in here. It was a bottle of beer blowing off. You couldn't put screw caps on it. You had to have a cork one because it used to blow when it fermented. But you'd lost your beer then, when it did that!

Dorothy Prince, housewife

Table   123

71 Old bottles, 2008 © Hannah Watson

I can remember me dad had told me about his grandmother, she'd used to make herb beer. The plants growing on the side of the road, one was called crosswort. His grandmother used to call it crackbottle because it would sharpen the beer and if it didn't have a strong bottom it'd crack it. I can remember that. You could buy Mason's Extract to make your beer when I was young and we used to make that. It were a good drink, nice for' hayfield and that sort of thing.

Harold Oven, farmer

Haymaker's Supper

Men would come and help in the hayfield just for a glass of beer and bread and cheese. My mother used to go at night down to the public house, with a big tall jug, bigger than that one that's in the window now, twice as big as that, and come back with it full of beer, and we had to go to bed before nine o'clock, because the men were coming out of the field for either boiled bacon or cheese.

Thomas Maltby, farmer

Home-made Elderberry Wine

I made it long enough before we were married, years ago, because it was before we came back up to Bakewell. And of course I must have a go at this elderberry wine. One of my brothers, he thought it was great. He had a glass or two and then in those days it was 'go out on me bicycle'. It was during the war; they went out with a couple of friends on the bikes. They ended up on the verge and they couldn't stop him laughing.

Margaret Mycock, farmer's wife

72 Working dinner – home-made food and drink in the field, c.1930s?
© Courtesy Angela Taylor

Deep Freeze

The trouble with growing things is that you can't eat them fast enough when they are growing. The house was pretty well freezing anyway. The dairy had big stone benches all the way around and it had an outside vent and a grill over the window so that it had fresh air. Of course when we had cows, milk went in there, but in the summertime it caused quite a problem keeping it, but in the wintertime it was freezing in our house.

Joan Stewartson, housewife

Preserves

Each farm had quite a few pantries and it was bottled fruit, wasn't it? Screw-topped jars, and they were big cool pantries with slab benches, stone benches. Many a time a salting bench for the pigs that were killed on the farm. You got all the fruit you could get really. It's remained with me because I've hated damson jam ever since, because damson seemed to be the only thing there was plenty of! My mother would have a big jam pan on top of the Aga cooker. Well, there was a big family like, there was always something. You had a lot of things off the farm. Poultry, pigs and lambs and whatever. You lived well.

John Eardley, farmer

Table   125

Salt

Beans and things like that you put into salt in soup cans and sweet jars - you sliced them first and layered them with salt. Gradually it turned to brine and that kept us with beans for quite a lot of the winter.

Joan Stewartson, housewife

Hanging Hams and Salting Pigs

People used to rear about three pigs, well depends if they'd got a litter, a sow having eight or ten pigs, they'd rear all those. Or if someone wanted to buy one, they'd sell them a little pig or two, whatever it was, if somebody wanted one for themself. And then my father used to have about four at once, and we'd kill one and he'd sell the other three to a pork butcher. All these farmers keep pigs because if they'd more milk than they could sell on the milk round or the dairies, and they didn't want to keep making a big rice pudding, they fed it to the pigs. It was an easy, economical way of both growing pigs and getting rid of surplus milk.

73 George Mellor salting a pig, History Live Exhibition, 1999 © Courtesy REAP

When you killed the pig at home, they'd arrange for the butcher to come and he'd kill it. You'd hang it up for two or three days, then he'd come back one night and cut it all up to salt it. There were salting back benches, big stone slabs and you'd salt it. You'd rub the skin of the animal and you kept rubbing it until you could feel some heat come through your hands, and that let you know that it was salted enough. You'd build up the friction and the salt. You could buy blocks of salt and you'd crush it with a rolling pin, just smash it all up and put it on and keep rubbing it into the skin. When your hand got hot, then you could feel the heat coming through, through friction, then that would be going into the meat, wouldn't it, the heat, and that'd do it.

You'd do it with one application, But the hams wanted a little bit more doing because you'd got bigger depth of meat to go into, hadn't you? On the hams, because the hams are pretty thick, you put saltpetre in the middle on the bones so, that, it helped to cure it. And the face, they call it the chall, the pig's face, underneath the pig's face, its jaw, everything like that, that was only lightly salted and you could eat that first. That would be ready in a week. The bacon took about, oh, a fortnight, something like that. The hams would take a little bit longer to cure. You'd get a pillowcase and put the ham in it and all the farmhouses had got hooks, and you'd just hang it up on the hook in a pillowcase, and just keep taking it down and cutting so much off it.

Thomas Maltby, farmer

Waterglass

Waterglass was a way of preserving eggs. It was horrible. I was terrified of it. We had a big mop bucket, one of those big open things – galvanised – and it had this stuff in and the eggs went into it. It actually sealed the shells of the eggs I think. So if you wanted any eggs you had to put your hands into this nasty slimy stuff. It was sort of whitish and you couldn't really see what was in it. I was terrified of it – I couldn't fetch eggs out of waterglass. But it did keep them for quite a while.

Joan Stewartson, housewife

Remedies

Cure-all

People used to have boiled onions and they was a cure-all for everything. My granny used to say if onions were a pound a pound, people would eat more. I knew a lady whose husband was an undertaker and when he got a nasty undertaking job, he came home to boiled onions to clear his stomach out ... I still like boiled onions today. What else did they have? They used to have goose grease to rub your chest with. You'll have heard that of course, too, as a cure-all.

Thomas Maltby, farmer

Table 127

Comfrey

I can remember having a sprain on my leg and the doctor came round and he would wrap some comfrey around that and bandage it up and that was a big recipe, comfrey. It's still grown today but I don't think people use it now like they did.

Harold Oven, farmer

Honey

I think it's a growing market because people are becoming more aware of the benefits of local honey and the claims that it helps combat hay fever, asthma and all these sort of things. Now whether that's proven or not, I don't know, it's not for me to say, but people have tried it and found it works. There are reasons why. For example, with hay

74 Comfrey, 2008
© Damian Hughes

fever, where people have an allergy to local pollen, the local pollens are still active in the honey that we sell because we don't sterilize the honey. They reckon, as people are ingesting them, their bodies are actually building up immunity to the pollen in a non-irritant way, so that when it does become air-borne, their body is more able to cope with it. It makes sense to me. I've also had people try putting honey on sores and cuts. They reckon that helps because it actually seals it and stops the air getting in. It also has antiseptic and anti-bacterial properties so there is that too.

Mark Dennison, beekeeper

Iodine

We sold cough mixture, but I can't remember us making any. We used to have iodine lockets on a string which you had to wear in winter and it had a piece of cotton wool soaked in iodine. I don't know what that was supposed to prevent. You used to soak your feet in mustard and water, a mustard bath, and that was to prevent a cold, I think.

Joan Stewartson, housewife

Lemon Barley

I used to get a chill on my kidneys and I used to be delirious and all this rubbish come up. And my mother used to boil barley, and I used to have to drink the water off the barley, and she used to put in lemon juice so it tasted a little bit better.

Thomas Maltby, farmer

Pobs

There's an old lady I did go to the other week and I said, "How are you?"

"Well, I haven't been very well." she said, "I'm a little bit better than I was. I went back to me mum's old thing."

"What was that?"

"Pobs."

Bread and warm milk. You warm the milk, break the bread into it and eat the bread and milk and it's pobs. They call that pobs here in Bakewell.

Pauline Jackson, milk lady

Sulphur

We used to periodically stove the place every year. We would burn sulphur in a tin and it would stink for days but I suppose it got rid of the vermin that was around the place. I know my mother in law used to treat sore throats with sulphur powder. You had to roll it up into paper and put it in your mouth. Then your mother blew it into the back of your throat.

Joan Stewartson, housewife

I can remember flowers of sulphur mixed with treacle. It was supposed to clear your blood out at spring time. And Epsom Salts were a cure for everything. Anything that was wrong with you, you had a dose of salts. Anything that tasted nasty was good for you.

Wilf Oven, farmer

At Table

Oh my mother and father always gave us good food - the table was the thing that mattered. Good pieces of beef and lamb and cheeses and everything was home done, home cooked and came from her mother obviously.

Jean Brocklehurst, famer's wife

Cooking smells are always very good aren't they, to get you started and ready for a good meal. They might be a bit dictated to, according to work on the farm, but in the past farming communities will have stuck more rigidly to meal times. I think farmers would still be good at coming in to sit at table, and children'd be expected to sit at table. It's a very good situation for discussing any family matters or anything else anyone wants to talk about. Family can be there to have a discussion, whereas if everybody disappears to their own rooms and wants

Table   129

75 At table: Blackwell Hall Farm tea c.1940s
© Courtesy of Angela Taylor, from the Gregory Collection

76 'The Sunday Meal': A farming family today still eats together, 2005
© Tom Jolley, Courtesy of the photographer and REAP

their food on a stool, or on their laps or whatever, the opportunity is missing. You can see exactly what your children are doing with the food; what and how much they are eating and it's important, you know.

I think it's a great shame to see younger generations who don't do that. In many households now there isn't a set time. Somebody'll come in, feel hungry and help themselves but no one else, before going to do something else by themselves. So it's not as sociable. That's a sad thing.

Tony Kemish, farmer

Home Economics

We have always eaten to live. Yet the price of food hasn't inflated along with the rest of everything else and it's people's expectations, lifestyles, shopping... the power of the retailer, basically. I think I'm correct in saying that it's dropped below ten per cent a household spends in a week on food out of their wages. They spend less than ten per cent to live and they'll probably pay about forty per cent on their mortgage. There was also the thrift factor, which was one of the crusades I was on when I was on the Sheep Strategy Council, but we lost the battle. They stopped the Home Economics and cooking came off the school curriculum about three generations ago and so you've got second and third generation mothers that have no clue how to cook. In fact they are frightened to death of it. The supermarket is anonymous, whereas, when they went into their local butcher or whatever, he would tell when they first got married, he would explain how to cook it and all the rest of it. And the mothers taught them. I remember there being five or six butcher's shops in Ashbourne. I think there are two now or one apart from the supermarkets. We'd have five or six in Bakewell, it's down to two plus the supermarket. Today you've got grannies who can't teach children how to cook.

Ian Lawton, livestock auctioneer

Status

I forget the precise figures, but not many years ago three-quarters of an entire village were working on the land in one way or another, whether as a blacksmith or people out in the fields. I was speaking to a chap the other day who remembers looking across a field and there were sixty-four people working and now it's one man and a tractor. It's inevitable with mechanisation, you've gone from 70 – 75% of people in rural areas to less than 2% employed in agriculture. A lot of the people who are living in the villages now don't know anything about agriculture, whereas before, they were involved in it. They knew farmers provided food and employment. Today farmers are too often seen as the man who drives round always covered in muck, making a mess on the roads. Other

Table   131

people sometimes don't see the other side of things.

Russell Ashfield, National Trust

Town and Country

I think for young people, for the thirty-somethings as well, they don't have the same connection with food. I mean, we knew where the meat was coming from because there was the carcass hanging in the shop. If you wanted a chop he'd take it down and he'd chop it up, so you knew where it came from, you knew how it worked, which I think subsequent generations have lost, which is serious because the connection isn't made. I've got people at the gate, with the livestock on the drive, and people don't know how to get through, which I find kind of strange. They don't know how to move the cattle. They think the cattle are going to go for them, which is the last thing on the cattle's mind. It's the disconnection between the countryside and people. Somebody a few years back said – they were talking about something not actually connected with this – said "the rural English man has more in common with the African peasant than he has with somebody living in Wolverhampton", which is probably true. There is a massive gulf between the town and the country.

I think we look at things differently, I think we look more long-term with things, because if you are dealing with livestock, you're putting a cow in calf, she's not going to calf for another nine months. If you're finishing cattle, you're not going to be finishing for another two and a half years, so you're thinking long-term. That's a big difference. It's understanding how the natural world works and having a stake in the community. Farmers were considered valued members of society. I was going to say that now they're not, but I don't think that's necessarily true. There has been a time, what ten years ago, when it was quite the opposite, and you daren't say you were a farmer, because farmers were perceived to be spongers off the state. They were perceived to be filling all their animals with drugs. And, possibly, it was farmers' fault to some extent, because they didn't stand up and say, "No we don't."

But I think the tide's turning. It was probably Foot and Mouth. Although it was awful, it actually turned people's perception, and made everybody understand that perhaps they weren't doing it like that. So I think that's helped.

Sue Jackson, farmer

Chatsworth Farmyard – a view from the late eighties

Parties of schoolchildren have come round the house since bus transport was available, and by the early 1970s thousands came each season.... We considered long and hard how children could be taken round a farm: on trailers behind tractors, perhaps, to watch the afternoon milking and end up with a glass of milk

77 Chatsworth Farm Yard, 2006 © Chatsworth Estate

and a slice of real bread and butter. It was a lovely idea but quite impractical. The distances are huge. Trailers, draped in children, travelling on main roads is not the best plan, and so we had to think again. As for the idea of drinking 'raw' milk straight from the cow, that is now said to be so dangerous that we should be had up for attempted murder.

A solution was found in the old Building Yard. It is out of sight in Stand Wood, but next to the house car park, so visitors are already very near to it. We decided to gather a cross-section of our farming and forestry operations in and around these buildings. Everything could be seen in a reasonable time, and people with enough energy could park their car for the day and see the house and garden as well.

The Duchess of Devonshire
The Estate: A view from Chatsworth, Macmillan 1990 p63-64

Apparently, when mum was little, they had rationing, so that's obviously changed. And I think that, before, people went to the supermarket and stuff because it's cheap and easy, but nowadays, people are slightly more into where their food comes from and if it's good, or if it's like really bad. Because, like, McDonalds, the food is awful and loads of my mates say they won't eat McDonalds now. Whereas when I was little it was just like, 'Yeah, McDonalds!'.

Erica Jackson, fourteen year old daughter of Sue Jackson

TABLE 133

77 Children making the most of the Farm Yard, 2008 © Fred Watson

Partners

The Peak District Food Heritage Project

This book has been produced as part of the Peak District Food Heritage Project, funded by the Heritage Lottery Fund.

Through this project, the Farming Life Centre has collected and recorded a huge amount of invaluable information and anecdotes about the food heritage of the Peak District. In our fast changing world, we hope the resulting book, audio material, and archive will become a valued historical resource for present and future generations.

Extracts from the interviews and a whole host of information about the project and the stories and resources collected can be accessed on-line at: www.thefarminglifecentre.org.uk/seasons_to_taste.

Essential to the success of the project have been the partner organisations, who between them have guided and managed the work involved in collecting the memories and putting them into the format you see here. These are: The Farming Life Centre, Read On – Write Away! East Midlands Oral History Archive and David Fine.

The Farming Life Centre

The Farming Life Centre was set up in 2004 to improve the quality of life of the Peak District hill farming community and to celebrate the farming way of life, past, present and future. Its premises at Blackwell Hall Farm opened in 2005 and since then, with the support of many partners, it has developed a range of initiatives all designed to offer opportunities for farming people to improve their health, and personal, social and economic well-being. It is a place where farmers and rural people young and old can meet with like-minded peers, and feel welcome and at home.

Me and my wife actually met because of the Farming Life Centre way back six or seven years when I was at the Peak Park and I was involved in this whole project as it started and we were looking for a venue with potential. I'd already done some work up here at Blackwell Hall Farm with Bill Gregory with some diversification of his buildings in the yard here and so I suggested, with others, that this building would make a perfect base.

I've always kept an interest in it because my background is in farming and now, as of January I've become the honorary Treasurer so I've got an active involvement again which is really nice – it's just such a fantastic resource and such a fantastic place. We've got three members of staff who are taking a whole host of projects forward, about food, health, diversification, as well as providing somewhere for farmers and people interested in farming to meet and talk. It's really exciting to see, having just started from a few people having a thought around a table

One of the projects I'm really excited about is Future Farms, which is looking at helping farmers in the Peak District diversify. It's not providing grant aid because there are other bodies doing that but there was nobody providing help and advice and a little bit of a guiding hand really. Farming can be quite an isolated way of life – if you are down a farm track and you are milking cows twice a day you don't go off the farm and so you don't actually see what others might be doing. Future Farms's about getting people together and talking through their experiences so they can move forward into the future. It's been so worthwhile that with my Treasurer's hat on we can maintain the funding to keep the Farming Life Centre going – we are supported by so many people now I'm hoping it's a given.

Russell Ashfield, Treasurer, The Farming Life Centre

The Farming Life Centre
Blackwell Hall Farm
Blackwell
Nr Buxton
SK17 9TQ
Tel: 01298 85162
www.thefarminglifecentre.org.uk
e-mail info@thefarminglifecentre.org.uk

Read-On Write Away

Read On – Write Away! is an independent partnership which aims to improve literacy and basic skills in Derbyshire and Derby City. Over the last 11 years, ROWA! has developed a community literacy and basic skills strategy based on a 'cradle to grave' approach, working closely with local partners. Targeting areas of high social need, ROWA! works with the key players in local communities, as well as strategic bodies at local, regional and national levels. ROWA! includes schools in its community literacy strategy, whilst emphasising the family as a vehicle for learning. From the outset, the emphasis has been on learning as a 'fun activity' and celebration of achievement at all levels. ROWA! has developed an expertise in the training and management of volunteers, who consistently give of their time and skill to play an invaluable role in ROWA!'s work, especially with socially excluded young people. The partnership with The Farming Life Centre came about because of the reputation ROWA! has for working with volunteers and led to this fascinating oral history project. As always, the plaudits should go to the volunteers who have spent hours interviewing, editing and photographing without reward except that of being part of the team which has produced this book.

Tony Faulkner, Volunteer Manager

Read On – Write Away!
01246 204851 ext 305
www.rowa.org.uk   e-mail info@rowa.org.uk

East Midlands Oral History Archive

The East Midlands Oral History Archive was originally funded by the Heritage Lottery Fund to establish the first large-scale archive of oral history recordings for Leicestershire & Rutland. The recordings are deposited in the Record Office for Leicestershire, Leicester & Rutland. The project's website has a searchable catalogue and a wide range of online resources for both schools and the public. EMOHA has also generated new oral history recordings through its own programme of interviewing, and provides advice, training and support for community groups, museums and heritage organisations, students and other individuals who are interested in developing their own projects. EMOHA is a partnership between the Centre for Urban History at the University of Leicester, Leicestershire County Council and Leicester City Museums and Library Services.

Colin Hyde
East Midlands Oral History Archive
Centre for Urban History
University of Leicester
LE1 7RH
0116 2525065
www.le.ac.uk/emoha email: emoha@le.ac.uk

David Fine

After previous careers in archaeology, education and social work, David Fine is a fifty-five year old writer who has lived in Bakewell since 1992. His work ranges from a humourous book about the French Revolution to being the poet-in-residence on the last Ashes tour to Australia, and includes both a history of Sheffield and a thriller, *The Executioner's Art*, set in Sheffield. "For a writer and poet used to working entirely on their own from material within to create poetry and fiction, *Seasons to Taste* has been a strange project, relating oral history to the printed page as part of a small and highly enthusiastic team. I wouldn't have missed it for the world."

4 Pickford Villas,
Monyash Road,
Bakewell
DE45 1FG
Tel: 01629 812075
e-mail: david@fineandandy.co.uk

Index of Contributors

Richard Gill, farmer: "*I am a stockman. You know on my gravestone I hope it will say 'stockman.'*" Pages 23, 94.

Bill Gregory, farmer: "*There was no building erected here from 1863 till 1968.*" Pages 15, 45, 61.

Christine Gregory, farmer's wife: "*I think as I mentioned to you before it doesn't really belong to me, the recipe.*" Page 115.

Albert Hall, fishmonger: "*Presentation was important.*" Page 91.

Jill Horton, farmer's daughter: "*It's part of how we live our lives and it's very important to me.*" Pages 27, 109, 121, 122.

Pauline Jackson, milk lady: "*Milk tastes and keeps better in glass bottles too.*" Pages 3, 102, 107, 128.

Sue Jackson, farmer: "*There is a massive gulf between the town and the country.*" Pages 14-15, 30, 32, 40, 58, 66, 79, 87, 107, 131.

Erica Jackson, Sue's daughter: "*I've got my own flock of hens.*" Pages 15, 102, 132.

Michael Jordan, restaurant proprietor: "*People eat with their eyes.*" Page 95.

Tony Kemish, farmer: "*Managing risk is something that farmers have always had to cope with.*" Pages 17, 29, 74, 119, 128.

Ian Lawton, livestock auctioneer: "*When the Milk Marketing Board was formed in the thirties it gave security.*" Pages 20, 28, 53, 58, 67, 105, 130.

Thomas Maltby, farmer: "*It's a fourteen day week.*" Pages 51, 118, 119, 123, 126, 127.

Margaret Mycock, farmer's wife: "*I've made oatcakes right up until recently.*" Pages 102, 116, 121, 123.

William Mycock, farmer: "*Used to grow everything, enough for the three households.*" Page 102.

Roy Mycock, master butcher: "*We've got a lovely shop. Fantastic custom, fantastic people.*" Arnold Mycock & Sons, High Class Family Butchers, 1 Scarsdale Place, Buxton. Tel: 01298 23330. Page 88.

Alec Neville, gamekeeper: "*People don't really poach any more, but having said that...*" Page 83.

Wilf Oven, farmer: "*Anything that tasted nasty was good for you.*" Page 52, 106, 128.

Harold Oven, farmer: "*It's no way to make a living unless you have a big acreage.*" Pages 19, 123, 127.

Index of Subjects

Index of Places